I0188645

Dear Proverbs 31 Woman... Stop Making Me Look Bad!

7 unshakable truths to reignite your passion for authentic spiritual growth.

By Kelly A. Foster

Dear Proverbs 31 Woman...Stop Making Me Look Bad!
7 unshakable truths to reignite your passion for authentic growth.
By Kelly A. Foster

Photography by Michael Henderson

ISBN-13: 978-0-578-91346-9

Manufactured in the United States of America

To those individuals who demonstrate a sometimes messy, but real life example of Christ. Those who love and keep on loving, give and keep on giving, support and keep on supporting no matter what. To the ones who see (horaó) me, whom I'm honored to call family; this is for you.

Table of Contents

I feel that it's necessary to give you a little information before we begin this journey. In true Kelly fashion, I must give you a bit of a disclaimer about what you are about to read. Have you ever found yourself feeling like you need to explain your actions, your words, your tone or intentions? What's behind the need to explain is often a feeling of being misunderstood. So you seek to get others to understand you better by explaining everything. You include details, motives, and your thought process all in hopes that you would be better understood. I know it's a terrible habit and isn't worth the stress. But here I am explaining to you my heart behind the words that will follow.

The journey of this book was birthed out of a study conducted in my Facebook group 'Imperfectly Purposed Women of God'. The women in this group wanted to go deeper into the study of womanhood and what better way to begin than with the Proverbs 31 woman. Or so I thought. Upon my initial studies, I had the hardest time trying to figure out what angle I could present this text in a group study that was not fake or discouraging. I was challenged because the feelings that came up for me when I read Proverbs 31 were nothing short of annoyance and defeat.

See, I am a self-proclaimed recovering perfectionist. Uber sensitive, freakishly creative; I sometimes think I am a super woman who can do it all (thanks, Mom). I'm quiet and reserved at first, but full of all kinds of cray cray once I'm comfortable. I like checklists, organized chaos, order, and flexibility. If that sounds like a hot mess to you, believe me it usually is.

Being from the Midwest (the Show me State to be exact), I'm a little country, a little rachet, and a whole lot of sassy. I am the queen of 'show me' and 'put your money where your mouth is'. Speaking of, my mouth has actually been known to get me into trouble a time or two. I'm pretty sure this book will too; but "well behaved women seldom make history", right?

See, Proverbs 31 wasn't sitting right with me. Although I can be prim and proper I'm also a little rough around the edges. In college I picked up an alias from my sorority sisters, Tough Love, and I've never felt more known and understood before. They called me Tough Love because I am fiercely loving and equally as tough on my loved ones. Not tough for no reason, but I am tough because I know that life will be tough on you.

I'd rather you have a firm friend that can walk with you as you live out truth than be hit with the realities of a rough life that you are ill prepared for. This book may be somewhat 'in your face' with my direct, sometimes firm words of encouragement. Think of me as your spiritual coach pushing you with relevant words of truth (maybe a few expletives), not filling your ears with useless fluff. Spiritual Squats all day!

I love hard, ya'll and let me be clear: if you are reading this I love you dearly. I mean it. I really do. Please take these words with love, grace, and truth. These are the words I've needed to push through the most challenging times of my life. Medicine doesn't alway feel good going down but it does its job. My prayer is that this book does the same for you. We need God's truth deep on the inside of our hearts.

As beautiful as you are, which you'll hear more about later, God desires your heart most. A heart that must be transformed and freed to live out His purposes for your life. Knowing who you are is the most important work you'll ever do. So I offer you my vulnerability, my transparency, and even my current struggles. Remember, I am walking with you on this journey. Sometimes yelling to push more out of you and sometimes wiping those tears. Girl, we got this!

Kelly Foster
St. Louis, MO

Makin' Me Look ~~Good~~ Bad Again

Dear Proverbs 31 Women,

Can you please stop making me look bad? I know I'm supposed to aspire to be like you and all but I just can't. My back hurts too much to bend down to play with my kids, my bathroom mirror has toothpaste splatters all over it, my business is not where I want it to be, and my neighbors barely know my name. My family doesn't sing my praises, they yell MOM as they search for mismatch socks through a pile of unfolded laundry on the living room floor. Or maybe it's still dirty? I can't keep track. My heels are ashy, my nerves are bad, and someone keeps hitting my already beat up old car. Seriously, girl if you could just shine a little less that would make me look a whole lot better. Thanks!

— Kelly

I mean really, the Proverbs 31 woman is nothing short of amazing. I love the way she's described in such detail. The way the scriptures take into account the many hats she wears and so eloquently illustrates how she's #crushingit in every single area of her life. She's the pillar of her family. She loves them well and it shows. She's trustworthy, devoted to her faith, she works hard and plans ahead. The Proverbs 31 woman is fiscally responsible and doesn't concern herself with gossip because she's too busy uplifting those around her with wise words and humble service. She's the epitome of what a Godly man should look for when choosing a wife. She's also the desired vision of every Christian woman who seeks to live God's way.

Before we really delve into this book and I begin to embarrass myself by sharing the quirky, sometimes repetitive stories God tells me to share, let's take a look at Proverbs 31 verse by verse.

This portion of Proverbs comes at the end of what some call the most wisdom filled book of the Bible. This chapter begins by giving the reader insight to the inspiration and motivation of the text to follow. Specifically, these are the words of King Lemuel as taught by none other than his mother. Now we don't know much about King Lemuel, he isn't mentioned much anywhere else in the Bible. Biblical scholars debate about who he actually was, supposing it was another name for King Soloman. For our intent and purposes, and to spare you the back and forth theological exegeting, we won't go there sis.

The point is, King Lemuel's mother, being rich in wisdom from years of knowledge and experience, took the opportunity as a mother to share her wisdom. In the 10 verses before we're introduced to our friend Ms. Proverbs 31 Woman, the king's mother warns him against such things as chasing women, depending on alcohol to get through life, and not standing up for injustice. All great advice right? Then she does what every great mother does, instead of leaving her son with a list of do's and don'ts she begins to tell him exactly what to look for in a Godly wife.

The last 22 verses of chapter 31 are meant to be a celebration of the virtuous woman. She's not an actual person but a set of amazing wifely characteristics. King Lemuel's mom doesn't want to leave it up to chance for her son to find a good wife, so she painted the most eloquent literary picture of her. You know, so he doesn't pick a hoochie mama.

This portion of the text is preceded by 30 chapters overflowing with what I like to call random wisdom. The essential theme of the book can be found in Proverbs 1:7. "Fear of the Lord is the foundation of true knowledge." Although filled to the brim with insight for every area of life, the Proverbs are better understood as general truths rather than doctrinal truths.

We can glean wisdom here but we need the Holy Spirit's guidance to know what's specifically appropriate for our individual situations. Make sense? Great!

Ok, so back to this celebration of a virtuous woman. Here's my verse by verse summary:

Vs. 10: Finding this virtuous woman is impossible without God. Just like wisdom, she can't be found without a genuine relationship with God.

Vs. 11: She's trustworthy. She adds to her husband's life in an invaluable way.

Vs. 12: She brings good, not harm. Her intentions are pure, not manipulative.

Vs. 13-14: She's a hard worker.

Vs. 15: She plans ahead, wakes up early, takes care of home first, and then she handles the concerns of those she's responsible for. (Balanced self-care)

Vs. 16: She understands the concepts of good business. She saves her money, gets informed, and then acts wisely to achieve her goal. The end goal benefits her entire household, not just herself. (Selfless)

Vs. 17: Her strength shows in all she does.

Vs. 18: She participates in work activities that are profitable, they add to her family and not take away from it. To make sure that her dealings are good she works hard and is even willing to stay up at night. (Persistence)

Vs. 19: She keeps busy by working, not gossiping or indulging in idleness. (Integrity)

Vs. 20: She helps the poor. She is charitable to those less fortunate. (Civic Responsibility)

Vs. 21: Her fears are minimized because of her wise planning, preparation, and trust in God. (Faith)

Vs. 22: She takes care of her outward appearance.

Vs. 23: Her honor brings honor to her husband. In the same way one's dishonor brings dishonor to her husband.

Vs. 24: She understands the needs of others and is able to add to her business by providing a service. (Understanding, & Empathy)

Vs. 25: Strength and Dignity. She lives and enjoys life without fear of tomorrow because of her trust in the Lord. (A Life Enjoyed)

Vs. 26: Wise speech, kind instructions. She's not overbearing, with an attitude, manipulative, or controlling.

Vs. 27: She takes full responsibility for her house.

Vs. 28: Her children bless her. Her husband praises her. They love her, appreciate her, and value her presence publicly.

Vs. 29: She is a great woman.

Vs. 30: Although beauty and charm are nice, what sets this woman apart is her reverence for the Lord. She fears God, which is the foundation of wisdom, thus her life looks like this. What empowers her to be virtuous is her fear of the Lord. (Character is greater than beauty)

Vs. 31: She is worthy of reward for her deeds.

Most Christian women are very familiar with the wife of Proverbs 31. We are reminded of her glory as we learn to be good wives, mothers, and women of the faith. The woman described within Proverbs 31 becomes who we aspire to be.

The depths of such an amazing woman of God and noble wife are described in very specific detail. From these short 22 verses, women from all over the world throughout history have sought to glean wisdom, understanding, and guidance to become women of virtue. In fact, I have torn through this text myself, looking, searching, examining what it truly means to be a virtuous woman. I've questioned myself and I've questioned God. What will it take for me to become like this woman?

This is a very high calling; to be a virtuous woman of God. This is a very high expectation. This is our ultimate goal as women of God, right? We want to be just like her; honored, loyal, responsible, respected, loved, and admired. Yet here I sit on the couch binge watching Netflix because some days I just don't feel like it. I should be praying. I should be volunteering. I should be sending over a freshly baked apple pie to my new neighbors but I don't. I desire the honor and praise of the Proverbs 31 woman but some days I feel lazy, unfruitful, and unproductive.

Ok, so maybe she will never get the letter I wrote but sis, my feelings are real. Have you ever felt this way as you read the text? Inadequacy mixed with jealousy and a hint of shade? I feel more challenged than inspired and I know I can't be the only one.

Most of us don't have the slightest idea about where to even start in becoming a virtuous woman. So, we seek out the text, we take notes, we study the words, we learn the attributes, and we try to BE virtuous. We make a list, set goals, commit to changing our ways, we make a vision board, and add to our prayer list. But to no avail, like clockwork, we fail. After all the list making and all the goal setting and all the good intentions-something holds us back.

You get discouraged. You stop trying because really you're just going through the motions, expecting huge results without really doing the work. You feel unsupported and unmotivated. You lose your drive. You get angry. You feel unappreciated. You completely disconnect from the Proverbs 31 role model. The more you try, the more you see that YOU and HER are not the same and it becomes obvious that WE, my friends, have a problem.

Sheesh! Why is this woman making me look so dang bad?

I see my obvious imperfections. I sulk in my lack of support, minimal resources, and unfruitful surroundings. Deflate because of a messed up childhood, lack of positive influences, and a broken home. I look at the Proverbs 31 woman and realize that SHE is virtuous and I am very far from it. Not only do we begin to feel far from her, but we don't even have the slightest clue of how to get back there and no vision of the path.

Your husband is not respectable, the kids are ungrateful little crumb-snatchers, there are no loyal friends to be found, no one will give your new business of the week a chance, and your patience is running oh so very thin.

How am I supposed to be a virtuous woman of God when I feel so defeated? How can I be so poised, purposeful, equipped, treasured, responsible, faithful, loving, charitable, and trustworthy inside of this broken, used, and neglected body? Virtuousness isn't oozing from my inner worried self or my outward mom bod. And this C-section scar, let's not even begin to talk about how that ruined my bikini dreaming life. Oh the drama! I know, but this is how I feel sometimes.

If you can relate to this, please know that you are not alone. This is officially called "The Struggle" and honey it is REAL.

But before we give up on everything ladies, something tells me we must be missing it. There's got to be a missing link as to how the woman of Proverbs 31 could be so successful at being virtuous. Honestly, she must have had a secret, a special sauce, a cheat sheet, something. I find it hard to believe that a hardworking mother is anything but overworked and underpaid. Yes, I'm sulking just a bit.

Maybe she did have something special, something that made all the difference as she lived the virtuous life that we all long to have.

Here's the dirty truth: The wife of noble character described in Proverbs 31:10-31 didn't just wake up like this and neither did Beyonce. She's no more special than you or I. She's not perfect as much as we fantasize her to be in our minds and she definitely has flaws.

It sometimes feels as if this perfect and ideal woman was put there to make us women feel bad about ourselves, to shame us into being better women. Ladies, now you know this isn't true. We can be so stubborn we'll do the exact opposite of the expectation just to buck against the system. (Insert evil laugh.) So that's obviously not an effective plan.

Listen, the Proverbs 31 woman is not some unrealistic, high and lofty standard set up for women to never attain, yet die scratching to get to. She is not described in the holy scriptures to hold women down or make them feel condemned (**Romans 8:1**).

This amazing woman whom we all seek to be has SOMETHING. That something is so powerful that it gives her the ability to be a virtuous woman of God. What is that something you ask? That something, my friend, my imperfect but amazing woman of God, is The Truth. The woman described in Proverbs 31 was ONLY able to be virtuous because of the very valuable truth of who she was in Christ. The same is true for us.

Understanding who Christ is and who YOU are to Him is the key to virtuous living.

We are missing this truth in our hearts. We have to know who we are in Christ. As God's creation, His chosen vessels, as women of God. The divine truth of God tells us who we are in Christ and gives us the power we need to live. That is what makes the woman of Proverbs 31 so virtuous. She wasn't confused, deceived, or uncertain about who she was. She didn't let her flaws, failures, and past broken relationships dictate how she saw herself. She believed what God said about her.

The good news today is that armed with the truth, you and I can be just like her. Ok, maybe not just like her but our own best version of ourselves. A version that knows without a doubt that God is who He says He is and nothing about our position with Him or His love for us will change. Friends, we are His. Imperfect, yes, but still His. Imperfectly His.

The virtue spoken of in Proverbs, a lot like salvation, doesn't simply come from the virtuous acts we do. It doesn't come from learning to behave virtuously. Virtue is not just a set of skills acquired over time that mean you're a better Christian. No, that's not the truth. And ladies that's not how we are ever going to be virtuous women of God.

Virtue is instead, a gift from the Lord. A gift? Yes, a gift! We don't work for it, we don't do anything to get it, we don't save up for it, we don't sacrifice for it. It is simply ours! We *are* virtuous because of Christ's work on the cross. Just as we are righteous because of Jesus' sacrifice on the cross. The death, burial, and resurrection of Christ settled our outstanding, overdrawn, and delinquent account on everything.

He not only bought our salvation and eternal life, but His death also paid for our ability to live this life better. By no longer being slaves to sin, we can now turn from sin and enjoy peace, love, joy, and grace that flows from God. These are all gifts purchased by Christ and virtue is no different. Christ gifted us salvation but we still have to work it out in our everyday lives **(Philippians 2:12)**. Similarly, Christ gave us virtue and we have to learn what it means to activate and walk out virtue in our everyday lives.

Walking out virtue, just as walking out your salvation, occurs when we submit our whole selves to Christ knowing that there is no greater wisdom outside of Him. It is from that reverence, that awe, that love (from Christ) that we then have the power to be the women He called us to be and do life according to His instruction. It's His power and not our own that helps us to live our lives **(Philippians 2:13)**.

So the question isn't "am I virtuous?" or "how do I become virtuous?" Nope, the real question is "do I really understand how valuable the gift is that I received from Christ?" You know that you are saved and because you've accepted Christ as Lord you have access to eternal life. But do you know that God doesn't have to just keep you by default? Like the extra cookie in a $5 Biggie bag at Wendy's. You're not some consolation prize given after all the good stuff has been won. No, you are the prize. You are very important to Him. You are valued and you have purpose despite what you've been through.

I believe that none of us can live up to our full potential as virtuous women of God until we know deep in our hearts who we are to God. We must realize that Christ chose us for His good purpose and works on our behalf daily, not because He has to but because He wants to. We are beautiful, precious, loved, and treasured by a holy God and until we know that deep down in our hearts, that valuable truth can be shaken by the enemy. Although saved, set free, and eternally restored to God, we can be deceived into thinking we're not enough and God doesn't really love us. Especially when a troubling sin seems like it just won't go away; you fall deeper and deeper away from God trying to "get it together" when all He wants is a broken heart to come to Him for repair.

This is not our destiny. This is not our truth. God never intended for us to walk around NOT knowing who we are in Him. It was so important that He decided to leave us a love note: 66 books long. And laced all throughout this love letter are the confessions of His love and feelings for us. So we owe it to Him to read these truths, confess them over our lives, and pray that they never be shaken again by the enemy's plots. And we owe it to ourselves to know these powerful truths and to never be deceived again.

Before we can examine the Proverbs 31 text we must begin with the truth of who we are in Christ. In this book you'll find 7 major truths that every follower of Christ needs to know & believe in their hearts. Depending on where you are in your journey, knowing these truths will ignite or reignite a fire inside of you propelling your spiritual growth. These truths provide a context; and with that proper context in mind, we can then begin to unfold the characteristics of virtue that make this noble woman an inspiration to all. At the end of each chapter I'll highlight the main points to remember as well as show you how to apply these points to your life realistically with daily actionable steps.

By the end of the book you'll also learn to R.E.S.T. in Jesus; a four part strategy to help you remember the principles of this book. R.E.S.T. will help you move from striving to doing productive & purposeful things with grace. You'll no longer feel guilty or ashamed about how your imperfections get in the way of your doing. Instead, you'll learn to R.E.S.T in Jesus' grace while giving it to yourself for a change. This is not an impractical book with random to-do lists and assignments just to pass the time, instead, armed with the belt of truth, you'll be empowered to be the woman of God that you ARE right now.

But maybe you're not a Christian. Maybe you stumbled upon this book by accident and your curiosity or my wonky rhetoric has kept you reading. Either way, it's nice to make your acquaintance and if you have a minute to spare I have some good news that just might interest you.

See, I've written this book from a believer's perspective. It includes so many powerful promises that God has given those who trust Him. I'd love for you to be a part of this big messy family. It's probably a lot like your own. You may have heard Christians are perfect. Nope, we're not. You may have heard Christians are judgy, yep we can be. But did you know that despite the flaws (we've got plenty) God loves us still. Here's why:

In the beginning, God created mankind in perfect relationship with Him **(Genesis 1:31a)**. Adam and Eve, the first man and woman, were given instructions from God not to eat of the tree of knowledge of good and evil **(Genesis 2:17)**. Instead, they ate the fruit they were forbidden from eating and this is known as mankind's first sin. This separated them from God and caused sin to enter the world through their bloodline **(Romans 5:12)**. This "sin bug" was passed down to mankind and as a result all of us are sinners **(Romans 3:23)**. Yes, I know such a bummer but it's true. We've all done something wrong. God is a Holy God and because of Adam and Eve's sin, God and mankind were separated **(Isaiah 59:2)**.

This was a huge problem but God had an even bigger plan to solve it **(Philippians 2:6-8)**. The Bible teaches us that the wages of sin is death, but the gift of God is eternal life **(Romans 6:23)**. See our huge problem, the separation between mankind and man, could only be solved by the shed blood of a perfect sacrifice. So in response to our new sinful condition, God sent Jesus Christ, His only Son, as the only perfect sacrifice to die in our place **(John 3:16)**. Jesus paid our debt by dying on the cross **(Matthew 9:6-7)**. He rose 3 days later, just as He said He would, with the power to free all of mankind from the curse of sin and finally give us a way to reconnect with God **(1 Corinthians 15:3-5)**.

The only way to God is through His Son, Jesus **(John 14:6)**. I know that feels offensive, but it is true. Thankfully what Jesus did on the cross gives us another option other than death. No longer are we slaves to sin, having no other way to go. If you turn from your sins by believing in your heart and confessing with your mouth that Jesus is Lord and God raised Him from the dead **(1 John 1:9)**; then you will be saved **(Romans 10:9)**. It's our redo, our second chance to have a relationship with Christ. We are promised forgiveness, reconciliation with God **(Ephesians 2:19-20)**, and eternal life (**John 3:16**).

Friend, if you have not accepted the Lord Jesus as your savior, or you are not sure if you are saved, pray this prayer with me:

God, I repent of my sins to You today as humbly as I know how. I confess that I believe that Jesus Christ is Your Son, He died on the cross for my sins. God, I want Jesus to come into my heart and be the Lord of my life. Thank you for Jesus' sacrifice and the ability to have a relationship with You. Lord, please seal it with the promise of Your Holy Spirit to guide me, in Jesus' name, amen.

If you just prayed this prayer for the first time, you are now a part of God's family! I am so overjoyed!! Please be sure to send me an email so that I can pray for you. Visit

KellyAFoster.com/resources for next steps and resources to jumpstart this new and exciting life with Christ.

Highlights:

- The Proverbs 31 Woman is #goals but we don't have to envy her. God has already given us what we need to be virtuous women of God.
- Your imperfections don't limit God's ability to use you.
- Virtue is a gift just like salvation. You don't do virtuous things to be virtuous, you are virtuous because of Jesus' work on the cross.
- Understanding who Christ is and who you are to Him is the key to virtuous living.
- With a clear understanding of the 7 unshakable truths you can walk out virtue in your life daily.

Virtue in Action:

- Begin each day in prayer. Create a list of things, people, and situations you want to pray about.
- Ask God to clearly show you the areas of your life that need a reboot.
- Discover your pain points. These are the areas of your life that cause the most stress, worry, and fear.
- Add your pain points to your daily prayer list.
- Listen as the Holy Spirit begins to reveal to you the daily adjustments you need to make in your life.

Two

You love me especially different

I was a junior in college when I experienced my first big heartbreak. I'll never forget the day I found out my on again off again 'boyfriend' had been seeing another girl. I remember the panic, my heart racing, the fear, the tears, and the devastation. The other girl contacted me and made it clear that whatever I had in my mind about our relationship wasn't real. In one moment it felt like everything changed. It didn't matter what he told me in the past. It didn't matter that he made future promises to me that had yet to come to fruition. It didn't matter that I believed his lies for years. That day I learned the good old fashioned hard way that love hurts, especially when it's with the wrong person.

Admittedly, he was a dud and not worth my tears as most first heartbreaks are, but 15 years later I am grateful for the lessons I learned because of him. But then again, those lessons had been brewing inside of me since childhood. I learned early on that love wasn't always helpful. It made people think less clearly, it often hurt very badly, and love was so dang uncontrollable. Full disclosure...I like being in control.

So it seems this heartbreak at 20 years old reinforced every faulty thing I learned about love in childhood while simultaneously setting me up to disbelieve my heavenly father's love for me. Double whammy for sure.

I've been a love skeptic and pretty much an all around cautious person for most of my life. I love the idea of love but for some reason my best examples were fake and only on TV. I still longed for love, even though I was deathly afraid of it. So I did what any rebellious young adult would; delved head first in this faux-love and completely gave myself over to the idea of love without truly knowing the giver of love. And of course when things fell apart I found myself disappointed, ashamed of my choices, and utterly confused about love. However, in this heartbroken place, God used my brokenness for good and I began to discover not just WHAT love is, but WHO love is.

I lost someone I thought I loved. That love hurt and wasn't something that brought goodness to my life. Sure it seemed great while I was in the dark but once the truth came to light the fun was over. Love isn't quick, fleeting, haphazard, and carefree. I longed for love, yet was scared to receive it. I sure didn't find it in the broke college dude who did me wrong. Realizing what wasn't love helped me to see what love is. Learning what love is drove me to the Bible.

I didn't have many verses under my belt at the time. I had not even discovered that Bibles came in various versions yet that were easier to digest. So when I clearly learned, accepted, and understood who God was from a King James Version of the Bible, I knew it was a miracle. A God thing. This was the single most pivotal truth that changed my life; learning that God is love **(1 John 4:8)**. After looking for love in all the wrong places, guys, clothes, shoes, beauty, acceptance, perfectionism, education, the church, sororities, books, music, my hair even; I found true love in Christ.

It is for this reason that I believe that everything begins and ends with love. The first step is realizing that God is love and although you could search all over to find a love, you'll never truly find it outside of Him. I could never feel completely fulfilled by anyone or anything's love. You see, I'm needy. I want what I want, especially from those closest to me (I'm the baby of the family so that's my excuse). Most of us hear that word and think negatively, but I've learned to embrace it. It's my truth and I serve an amazing God who's big enough to handle all my clinginess. I don't even feel bad telling you, because I know, of course, that you are needy, too.

You need love. You crave it. You look for it everywhere you go. Yeah, you might say you don't care what people think but deep down you long for an intimate relationship where you can be 100% you; raw, exposed, and unfiltered but still loved. You want that unconditional acceptance, that never ending love; but like me, you won't find it in stuff or people, in things or places. Move across the globe, change your career, go back to school, snag a new man, and that gaping hole on the inside of your heart is still empty until the unfailing love of Christ fills it up. As it turns out you don't need that man or that designer handbag. You don't NEED lashes to highlight those eyes or skinny jeans to accentuate those hips. What you and I need is something that we can't buy, wear, or marry; we need to know without a shadow of a doubt that the God we serve loves us immensely and is here to fill every hole of dissatisfaction and regret in our lives.

You are immensely loved by a Holy God.

Ladies, if we are ever going to walk out virtue in our lives and be the powerful women God has called us to be, then we must know, understand, and embrace this truth wholeheartedly. God loves us and there's nothing we can do about it. There's nothing we can do to make Him love us any less and there's nothing we can do to make Him love us any more. He just loves us period. We sure do try to get brownie points though huh? We think our good works, our volunteerism, our charitable giving, and our church work helps us maintain His adoration of us. That is simply not the case. God doesn't love us because of ANYTHING that we do and we can't ever separate ourselves from His love. Don't believe me? Still need some convincing? Well, let's examine the text. Let's see what the holy scriptures have to say about this great love that God has for us. What has God spoken that we can be sure of as we live our lives completely saturated by His love?

We can be certain that God loves us immensely. It's a love that is beyond our control, completely above our expectations, but well within our reach. The holy scriptures scream of His love for us from Genesis to Revelation. If we are walking around feeling unloved, it's not because God hasn't told us lately. We find His love deep within the text; richly rooted in the travels of Exodus, the devoted hymns of Psalms, and hidden in the wisdom of Proverbs. His love is buried in the grave of Mark, resurrected in the book of John, edifying in the 13 letters written by Paul and boldly proclaimed on the white horse of Revelation. We see God's love for us spelled out loud and clear, not masked, or covered up, but proudly proclaimed. Truth must be spoken, heard, and received. Simply knowing the truth with head knowledge is not enough.

So what exactly does the Bible say about God's love for you?

God's love for you is immeasurable.

"That he would grant you, according to the riches of his glory, to be strengthened with light by his Spirit in the inner man; That Christ may dwell in your hearts by faith; that ye, being rooted and grounded in love, may be able to comprehend with all saints what is the breadth, and length, and depth, and

height; and to know the love of Christ, which passeth knowledge, that ye might be filled with all the fullness of God" Ephesians 3:16-19 KJV.

There is simply no way that we can even begin to measure the love of God for us, His treasured children. There are no tools, no measurement that could contain the amount of love He has for us. It's impossible. In the scripture above, Paul encourages the church at Ephesus (and modern day believers, too) to understand just how significant it is for the believer to know God's love. In fact, according to Paul, being rooted in God's love will keep us strong in the faith. When we know, and I mean really know, in our hearts just how wide, long, high, and deep His love is for us, it gives us something supernatural to hold onto in this life.

God loves you, my sweet sister. He LOVES you. From the top of your pretty little numbered hairs head to the tips of your pedicured toes (or ashy toes like me). He loves you. And guess what's even better than that? God's love for you won't quit. It will never end. His love is so great for you that it literally cannot be measured or contained. This is not something that your struggles or temptations can take away from you. God's love for you is a fact. God says He loves us and He cannot lie. His promises are true and we can put our full trust in His word. Despite the circumstances of your life, He loves you. Plain and simple.

"Your unfailing love, O Lord, is as vast as the heavens; your faithfulness reaches beyond the clouds" Psalm 36:5 NLT.

The Psalmist even described God's immeasurable love by saying it is unfailing. God's love never gives up, His love reaches high beyond the clouds, and low even past the valleys. This means that no matter where you are, this limitless, immeasurable, unfailing love can always reach you. No mountain top success or bottom of the pit failures can take His love away. No sin, no pain, no past regrets. What an amazing truth to hold on to. When you are pressed on every side, being pulled by the numerous hats that you wear on a daily basis, this truth will strengthen and sustain you. When the weight of motherhood, marriage, work, single parenting, business building, school, and church become too much, we are comforted by scriptures like Ephesians 3 and Psalms 36. Scriptures like these encourage us to hold firm to who God is and how He feels about us.

"The Lord hath appeared of old unto me, saying, Yea, I have loved thee with an everlasting love: therefore with lovingkindness have I drawn thee" Jeremiah 31:3 KJV.

Oh, to be loved with an everlasting love! Can you just for a moment try to fathom what that really means? Here we are smack dab in the middle of time, as God's creation, with the task of living a very short life in the span of eternity. We are marred by sin, ravished by a fallen world, and subject to the principalities of darkness everyday. But God, in His infinite love, has chosen us to have a relationship with Him. He has vowed to be our God, He sustains the cosmos and the galaxy at just the right place so that we can have life. He's both life giver and sustainer, yet we are so unworthy. This God, the author of the universe, the transcendent, triune, Holy and perfect God of Abraham, Isaac, and Jacob loves us with an everlasting love. Not because of how good we are, but because it pleases Him to do so.

This is the firm foundation of His love that we place our trust in. A love that can't be added to or taken from and that my sister is the best kind of gift. God isn't like your messed up heartbreak situation, your former spouse, or ex-best friend. We don't ever have to pull teeth to get Him to define the relationship. His love is clear, His love is perfect, unending and never failing.

God's love for you surpasses any love you can ever experience on Earth.

"And we have known and believed the love that God hath to us. God is love; and he that dwellers in love dwellers in God, and God in him. Herein is our love made perfect, that we may have boldness in the day of judgement; because as he is, so are we in this world. There is no fear in love; but perfect lobe casteth out fear: because fear hath torment. He that earth is not made prefect in love. We love him, because he first loved us" 1 John 4:16-19 KJV.

It's not always easy to understand how a holy God can love a sinner like me and you. It can be even harder to accept His love as true when significant people in your life have let you down and not shown you the love that you craved. Even while reading this you may not feel loved. You may not feel cherished and cared for, but you have to trust God's truth even when your situational truth feels so real. Situations don't change God's love for you. Your feelings of worth or value do not have anything to do with God's truth. If you find yourself feeling a lack of love, you need to saturate yourself with the truth. Speak it daily, pray it, read it in the scriptures, journal about it, listen to music proclaiming it. Let the truth of His love infiltrate every crevice of your life. I like to write down how God feels about me and read it later when I need it most. Usually after an intense debate with my 5-year-old over pig newtons. (If you got that stale joke, lady you are my people.)

God loves you because He is God and some things we can never fully understand.

"My thoughts are nothing like your thoughts," says the Lord. And my ways are far beyond anything you could imagine" Isaiah 55:8 NLT.

Here's where the rubber meets the road and you have to have faith. We don't think like God. Our minds do not process information the same way that His does. At the center of our thoughts are sin and selfishness. We aim to please...ourselves. If it benefits us, and hopefully very quickly, then it's good. This simple way of thinking is nothing like God's. We are utterly, systematically, and intrinsically different.

We also don't act like God. Our motives to act come from our prideful, egotistical, and self-centered desires. We rarely put others first, we are slow to trust, and even slower to forgive after trust is broken. The attributes of selflessness, forgiveness, and righteousness are what make God who He is. God's actions are always righteous, holy, and just. Our actions are often misguided, deceitful, and biased. Even on a good day, I'm more inclined to drink Pepsi over water (Pray for me y'all).

So when we begin to try to understand exactly how God continues to love a broken people, we must completely understand that God is not a mere man. He is not subject nor slave to sin. He is divine and sovereign. Some things about His character we just won't get; it's simply because God is not like us.

God loves you because you are HIS.

"And the Lord, he it is that doth go before thee; he will be with thee, he will not fail thee, neither forsake thee: fear not, neither be dismayed" Deuteronomy 31:8 KJV.

You are the prized possession of God. You are His. He loves you now and He always will because you are His own. He promised to be with you. He promised to never fail or abandon you. God, who cannot lie or break promises, made a voluntary covenant to be with you always and He plans on NEVER breaking that promise.

"And say until them, Thus saith the Lord God; In the day when I chose Isreal, and lifted up mine head unto the seed of the house of Jacob and made myself known until them in the land of Egypt, when I lifted up mine hand until them, saying, I am the Lord your God" Ezekiel 20:5 KJV.

We all remember the Israelites and all their many, many failures with God. God gave a commandment, they broke it. God forgave them and renewed their covenant, only for them to break it yet again. This went on and on throughout the book of Exodus despite the consequences they faced. It's exhausting to read but imagine if you lived through it. I wonder how many times the Israelites thought to themselves, "Man, God won't forgive us this time," or "God will surely abandon us this time." But God, being rich in mercy and love, in His great wisdom with redeeming justice continues to fulfill the promises He made to His people so many years ago.

We are a lot like the Israelites, walking with the Lord but never fully understanding what it means to have Immanuel, God WITH us. God has made His home in our hearts and yet we think that God will abandon us for a newer, better, more obedient people. The truth is, He won't. No matter how much dirt we do, it can't change the love He has for us. No, He is not pleased with our disobedience. Yes, He might discipline us and allow us to experience adversities and challenges that will help us grow. But what He won't do, what He will never ever do, is leave us or stop loving us.

God loves you and there's nothing you can do to make Him love you any more and absolutely nothing you can do to make Him love you any less. In order to walk out virtue in our lives, to be the virtuous woman that God calls us to be and to stop feeling so defeated every time we read Proverbs 31; we must declare, accept, and embrace this truth about who we are in Christ.

Prayer:

Dear Heavenly Father,

Thank You for making Your truth clear. Thank You for looking beyond my pain, my trauma, my sin, and even my attitude to give me what I need most. God, thank You for Your love. God, let the truth of Your love fill my heart and my mind. Let Your words of truth comfort me and keep me when I do unloving things and I feel unworthy. Help me to seek validation in only You and to seek true love in only You. In Jesus' name, amen.

Highlights:
- You are loved perfectly by a Holy God.
- There is nothing you can do to make God love you more and there is nothing you can do to make God love you less.
- God's love for you is immeasurable.
- God's love for you lasts forever; it does not end.
- God's love for you is nothing like any other love you've known on Earth.
- You are His and there's nothing you can do to change that.
- God will never abandon you.

Love in Action:
- Begin each day with the affirmation: "I am immensely loved by a perfect God."
- In your journal, begin making a list "I feel loved when..."
- Add to your list as you get inspiration.
- Pray over your list and ask God to reveal to you any lies you are believing about love in general and His love specifically.

I Will Pursue

We now know that God loves us immensely and there's nothing we can do to add to or take away from that love. As women who seek to have virtue and honor in our lives, there are some basic truths we must also understand. We have got to know, with certainty, who we are in Christ. We can't be unsure and depend on the world and our culture to reiterate God's truths to us on a daily basis. Quite the opposite will actually happen. Day in and day out advertisements, magazines, social media, and reality TV will try very hard to place women in a box. This box is nothing reminiscent of God's plan for us. This box will leave us feeling alone, unknown, less than, and not enough. God never intended for His children to feel this way. God wants us to know the truth, not lies. That's why He left us the word of God. As we meditate on the scriptures, His truth is etched in our hearts and never plucked out of our minds by anything else.

The truth is, you are virtuous. Remember virtue, like our salvation, is a gift from God. Making a random list of virtuous things to do is not quite the way we become virtuous. We simply ARE virtuous. Not because we always act and do the right things, but because we are loved by God and intimately pursued by him.

I will never forget the day God showed me that I was pursued by Him. I remember the clothes I had on, the way my hair was, the feeling of the weather that day, the way the wind blew on my face as my big crocodile tears (as my mother says) wet my delicate and naive 20-year-old cheeks. Remember that relationship I was getting over in college; well you really couldn't even call it that. It was more like a really stupid "situationship" with a guy I knew I had no business being with in the first place.

So exactly how did one of the worst heartbreaks of my young adult life teach me anything about God's pursuit of my true heart? God used this situation to gift me an overwhelming blessing. For the first time in my life, I experienced God's peace. I instantly knew that He was with me, He had always been with me, and in spite of everything I did to reject Him, He wanted a real relationship with me.

The guy I had been dating had also been dating other girls, so of course I was crushed. It wasn't just because he lied or because he didn't take the relationship as serious as I did. Ultimately, I was devastated by this discovery because I had compromised myself for this guy. I reduced my morals, ignored my faith, and rejected every good thing that I had come to know as truth. I accepted the lie and rejected the truth and here I was left with nothing to show for it but regrets and crumbled tissues on the floor.

I cried for weeks. I literally wasted weeks of my perfectly flat stomach young life mourning the loss of my dignity and self-respect. Taking on shame I shouldn't have. Being overly responsible for actions that were not my responsibility. Questioning every decision I made. Going over and over again in my mind how this could be happening to ME. In the midst of my tears I remember crying out, "God, help me! Heal my broken heart." Probably the first time I had ever done this, so passionately, so seriously, needing something I obviously could never give myself. I was at the end of me. I was dejected, feeling low, the pain of my heart ached in my stomach, my chest, and throat. It was an internal heartache but the pain was palpable.

Now before you start feeling sorry for me, don't forget that I had knowingly rejected God and my former teaching during this time. I was grown-grown and acting grown, making all the decisions that I wanted to. Before then I convinced myself that I didn't really need God for everything. Some things I could figure out on my own. Like this situationship for example. Sisters, that was only the beginning of a series of "grown choices" that I was plain old wrong about. Being smack dab in the middle of this crisis made me see things so much clearer. Thank God for the crisis that brings about clarity and revelation. Remember: He will use even the painful situations for your good.

The act of crying out to God, unbeknownst to me at the time, was really a way for me to surrender my jaded thinking to Him and ask for help. For a type A personality, perfectionist young girl who thought she knew it all and heard it all, this was huge. In return, I received a special gift. Peace. I had never experienced anything like this before. My pain was still there, my situation unchanged, yet my heart was no longer troubled. I didn't feel the nagging pit in my stomach from anxiety or the ache in my throat from crying. I felt free. I could breathe. I could gather up the strength to leave my apartment to go to class. I didn't even feel the shame or embarrassment of having my business in the streets. I called out to God, I repented of my sin, and I asked Him to be to me what no one and nothing ever could; not even myself and He did it. (Won't He do it!)

That's the moment when I knew God was pursuing me. That's when I knew that there was no depth that I could go to that would ever separate me from His love or His pursuits. He loved the prideful, disrespectful me; He loved the one who abandoned His teachings, He loved the me that wasn't perfect and had lost her way.

To that me, the "bad" me, God gave calm to my storm. It was the lightness of His yoke that Jesus speaks about in Matthew 11:30. He says "come to me, all you who are weary and burdened, and I will give you rest. Take my yoke upon you and learn from me, for I am gentle and humble in heart, and you will find rest for your souls. For my yoke is easy and my burden is light." It just felt good to my soul. God's peace felt like a warm soothing bath, like a glass of cold water on a hot day, like the smell of Tide on freshly washed clothes. It was a tangible feeling of goodness like God was whispering "everything will be alright" to my very soul. That peace was the most amazing gift I've ever experienced before. The tears stopped, I could think straight again and although I was still hurt by the betrayal, I had hope.

That hope taught me that I could access the peace of God whenever I needed it by simply asking. It seemed to heal my wounds almost instantly. It cleared my mind, removed my fears, and set the reset button on my faith. I felt like an elder from the old school church that used to say, "I'm not telling you what I've heard, I know God is a healer because I've tried him for myself."

When I tried God, He proved Himself to me, not because He had to, not just because I asked Him to, but because He knew that if He did I would respond. He pursued me exactly how I needed to be pursued in order to draw me closer to Him. The same promise that was offered to me as a naive, 20-year-old know-it-all is the same promise that you have today. Everything we need is deep inside the will of God.

You are intimately pursued for a relationship with God.

Beloved, you are pursued by a holy God. That's probably the most flattering compliment any woman could ever have. But we don't always see it that way do we? We often mistake the compliments and flattery of a charming man to be more valuable than the truth of God's word. We want good morning texts instead of Gospel truth. God's word screams to us that we are called, chosen, and pursued by a faithful God. But we ignore it, don't we? We minimize it, we reduce it, and we even reject it altogether. But guess what? That still doesn't take any of the truth away from it. God intimately pursues us for a personal relationship unlike any other person on this earth ever can. He sees us exactly where we are, understands our needs, and calls out to us to provide for those needs, leaving us satisfied- thirst completely quenched in him.

Understanding God's pursuit of our hearts completely changes everything. So, what does it mean to be pursued by God? How exactly does God pursue us? Why is this pursuit so significant?

God does the pursuing, always:

We all came to Christ in different ways. Some grew up in the church, some were young adult seekers, some got lost and eventually found their way to Christ, others experienced a miraculous transformation. Some also might be what I like to call logical believers or knowledge believers. These are individuals who studied scripture, historical facts, and figures and did research until drawing the conclusion that Christ is the only way. No matter how you came to Jesus, the important fact is that by the power of the Holy Spirit you surrendered to Him. However, the way we came to Jesus impacts what we believe about Him. Some of us might even think we had something to do with us accepting Christ as Lord. Some might even be so foolish to think that they pursued the faith or turned to Christ. This can't be further from the truth. No matter how you come to Christ, it is He who pursues, always.

"Look! I stand at the door and knock. If you hear my voice and open the door, I will come in, and we will share a meal together as friends" Revelations 3:20 NLT.

We can be certain from this text that God is the one who in fact initiates and activates the relationship, not us. He stands at your door, He calls you by name, invites you to have an authentic relationship with Him. If and when you open the door, Jesus the Christ, Son of the living God will be standing there ready and willing to make a deep connection with you. Think about it, we don't invite just anybody into our homes, we don't share a meal with every person we meet on the street. We take people into our homes and offer to share a meal with them as a way to deepen the relationship and create a real friendship. This is exactly what Jesus promises us in His pursuit of our hearts.

Not only does Jesus call us out of darkness and into relationship with Him, but He also invests in us while we are sinners.

"But God, who is rich in mercy, for his great love wherewith he loved us, even when we were dead in sings, hath quickened us together with Christ, (by grace ye are saved;) and hath raised us up together, and made us sit together in heavenly places in Christ Jesus" Ephesians 2:4-6 KJV.

Through Christ we have the ultimate comeback story. There will never be another story of redemption, of rags to riches, of death to life greater than God's redemptive story of saving us through Christ. We live because He died. We commune with God because of His sacrifice. Jesus didn't do all of this because we are so honorable, obedient, and faithful. He was obedient to the father and glorified Him by keeping His commandment to be with us always.

Christ invests in us while we are still sinners. Jesus is not surprised or caught off guard when we struggle with past sins that keep creeping back up. He's not unaware that we have conflicting minds to serve God and to serve our flesh as we practice Christian living. Christ knew all of these things even before dying on the cross and yet He still made the ultimate sacrifice for us.

It reminds me of when my middle daughter, who was 3 at the time, took a bite out of each cherry in an entire bag of freshly bought cherries. One day after returning from the grocery store I was being #lazymom and didn't put up all the groceries, only the perishable items that couldn't wait. The plan was to take a nap with the kids and put the rest of the groceries away once we woke up. Well, my little middle daughter decided to fall asleep on the couch and wake up a bit early and take one bite out of each cherry. In her mind, she would't get in trouble because she didn't eat them all. There's nothing like a toddler story to remind you that you are just like a child to God.

Of course her parents woke up to find an entire bag of half eaten cherries (at $4.99 a pound might I add). She adamantly denied eating the cherries, so much so it was hard to keep a straight face. Even still, I pushed her until the truth came out. As her mom it made sense that once she saw those cherries they would be irresistible to her. I wasn't mad that she ate them, I just wanted her to know that nothing would change about our relationship if she told me the truth. Although she may get a consequence for eating the cherries, I would still continue to be her mother no matter what.

So why do we hide from God? Why do we run from Him when we face troubles? Why can we be so easily convinced that God doesn't love us or want us because we sinned? It's a lie! It's all a lie! As the old hymn says, "Jesus, knows all about our struggles" and He still wants us. We can never hide from Him because He is our ultimate pursuer, even as we deal with sin.

As God pursues us, He prunes and develops us:

Have you ever felt the weight or pressure of righteousness or doing good? Ever felt like the haters are getting over on you while you try to "act right"? Chances are you are being pursued by God. A key indicator we experience that confirms God's pursuit of us are trials.

Now let me be very clear, I am a firm believer in the biblical principle of reaping and sowing. A lot of us experience rough patches due to the seeds that we've planted in our lives. For example, you might feel persecuted when bill collectors call your house or your job but chances are when you dig a bit deeper you'll find a clear root to this problem. Making financial promises you know you can't keep and not paying your bills on time is directly related to experiencing past due notices in the mail and calls from bill collectors.

Before you side-eye me, I've been there before, too. However, I have to be real, this is not a situation of persecution for righteousness' sake. It's more than likely a result of the seeds of non payment that led to the bill collectors calls, sis. Let us not be foolish to believe that our own misguided choices are anyone's fault but our own. Yes, you can learn from these financial mistakes and do better but ultimately it is your own wrong doing that got you there. Deep Breath. That wasn't so bad.

Instead, when the Bible teaches us about experiencing trials and persecution for Christ's sake it's talking about something entirely different and due to no fault of your own. As we are pursued by God, He allows us to experience hardships that will grow us and prune us into the women of God that He calls us to be. This is how He develops us. This is how we know we're being pursued: Psalm 139 tells us, "You know me I cannot escape you. You see me You will judge the wicked. You will search & correct my heart so that I'm not among them."

"And not only so, but we glory in tribulations also: knowing that tribulation worketh patience; and patience, experience; and experience, hope" Romans 5:3-4 KJV.

Since we cannot escape the presence of God, and since we know He pursues us in this character-building process, we should not be surprised by the things we experience. The pruning process in plant growing requires the gardener to cut away from the very branches that he desires to grow. He must remove the browning leaves so they will not affect the healthy ones. If this process doesn't take place, the entire plant will eventually suffer and die.

When we go through a pruning process it can be very painful. But there is purpose in your pain. It's not meant to take you out but it's meant to bring you closer to the one who Is and Is to come. Something happens to our character as we experience hardship. We turn to God, we cry out, we seek Him, we pray, we trust Him, we give up our plans. For every branch, vine, and leaf that is trimmed, you are pursued. Your righteous self can grow even through the pain and thrive in Christ. The pruning process is an amazing growth tool used by God as He actively and intimately pursues us for a personal relationship with Him.

Remember me at 20? I knew who God was but wasn't acting anything like a follower of Christ. I wanted my way, no matter how physically, mentally, or emotionally draining it was. The reality is, we can see God's pursuit of us best in the midst of struggle. Even as I turned from Him and rejected His ways, God sought me out. He does the same thing for you.

But some of us reject Christ's pursuit. We ignore the spiritual connections and blame our hardships on the devil or haters when God intended it all for our good. How amazing is it to know that God has graced you for this time, this moment, this struggle, this success. We are not merely bystanders in life, being tossed to and fro because we don't know what to expect. Quite the contrary, God has given us guidance through His Spirit, power to do the impossible, and wisdom to understand our struggles. The real question is: Do you believe that you have been chosen, called, and pursued as a follower of Christ who CAN DO your life right now as it is? Well, even if you're not sure, God is. You have the power to walk out virtue in your life because you know who you are in Christ.

Despite the circumstances of your life, you are intimately pursued by God. You couldn't leave Him even if you tried. Turning from God isn't an option, running from your purpose in fear will never be successful, and trying to hide your sin in shame can't keep you from God. You are loved and you are pursued intimately.

Honorable and virtuous women don't just appear out of thin air. They also don't do a bunch of virtuous acts to make them better. These women are virtuous first because of their confidence in God's truth which is solidified in their hearts. Every good deed she does because of that "God-fidence" is merely the outward fruit that automatically flows from understanding who you are in Christ.

Prayer:

God,

You have pursued me intimately. You see my flaws, you know my struggles yet You still want me. Thank You for making me honorable. Thank You for seeing greatness in me and calling me higher. Help me to accept Your pruning process and see it as good. Strengthen me to be whole, healed, and spiritually mature by the power of Your Holy Spirit. In Jesus' name, amen.

Highlights:
- God pursues you.
- God initiates, sustains, and maintains the relationship.
- God invested in the relationship while you were still a sinner.
- God is pruning and developing you. It may be painful but it is beneficial.
- You can see God's pursuit of you best in the midst of struggles.

Pursuit in Action:
Meditate on the following questions:
1. Have you ever pursued someone or something?
2. What motivated you to continue pursuing?
3. How can you see God's pursuit of your heart in your life?
4. What can you do to embrace your struggles and see them as purposeful?

Power in the Blood

L et's take a moment to clarify some things so that we are all on the same page. Your value, your worth, the great gift of salvation from Christ as well as the virtue you have as a woman of God is not dependent on your WORKS; rather it is a GIFT from God. You are immensely loved. You are intimately pursued by a righteous and holy God. These truths fuel our behaviour and give you the power you need to be what it is that you already are: A woman of virtue.

The only problem is, sometimes you don't feel so virtuous. Sometimes you're not really aware of the power you have through Christ. Sometimes you self-sabotage, count yourself out, doubt your purpose, worry about the unknown, and fear failure. You essentially walk around fully equipped to live a life of faith with endurance and confidence in Christ but you act powerless, defeated, and ill-equipped. You question your existence and your entire relationship with God all because you don't fully understand how powerful you are to carry and conquer your heavy load in life.

This is the lie. This is the enemy's plan. Get you distracted by your surroundings, defeated by your situation, ashamed by your past and voila; just like that you're completely unaware of your strength and power in Christ. The very thing that God gives you to draw others to Christ, your story, will be the thing you despise and reject, keeping you further and further away from freedom in Christ.

Falling into the trap of these distractions happens every day, even in the mundane. It reminds me a bit of church on Sunday morning, before Coronavirus of course. I attend a fairly large church in St. Louis, Mo where the weekend church services can bring in several thousand people each week. My family attends the 11am "family" service. Let's just say this is probably the highest attended service of all 3 weekend services because of the excellent children's ministry.

Getting in and out of church during the 11am service is quite a challenge. The most interesting area to make it past are the double doors leading to and from the children's ministry. With this being the "family" service, lots of families, moms, dads, sisters, and brothers race back and forth; in and out of this door between 11-12. At the end of church there's usually a line at that door. Every single Sunday as I approach the double doors heading to the children's ministry I see that familiar line forming. One by one, parents stand behind one another, graciously waiting their turn to go through the door. Now remember, there are in fact two doors leading to the children's ministry, but for some reason every single Sunday, all the parents wait graciously behind one another for their turn to walk through one door.

Isn't it interesting that fully equipped adults will stand in a line one behind another waiting for something that they can have if they just step to the side and pull open the second door? How many times have we walked away from something in defeat, not because we are ill-equipped but because we lack the confidence and courage in our power through Christ?

As children of God, we walk around completely equipped by God to handle EVERY heavy load & good thing given to us. The problem isn't that we need more purpose or more power. The problem is that we need to deeply know and comprehend the purpose & power that we already have through Christ.

See, if we really knew the purpose and power that we have through Christ we wouldn't act the way we do. We wouldn't be taken out like we are, or discouraged, or overwhelmed like I tend to get at the thought of making dinner. Every. Single. Day. If we really understood who we are and whose we are, we would be able to stand against the devil's schemes as instructed in Ephesians 6:11.

But don't worry, sometimes all we need is a clear reminder to set us back on track. A truthful confirmation of God's plan and purpose for our lives so we can re-adjust and move boldly in the direction of His will for our lives.

God has a plan for each one of us:

"'For I know the thoughts that I think toward you, saith the Lord, thoughts of peace, and not of evil, to give you an expected end'" Jeremiah 29:11 KJV.

We are not arbitrarily moving about the earth by chance, waiting for the next random act of the universe to have an effect in our lives. On the contrary, we were created by an infinite God, birthed with a purpose, and sustained by the miraculous works of His hand. You are a purposed woman of God. There is a plan for your life. That plan exceeds your past struggles, current misfortunes, and even your future fears.

As children of God we are not subject to coincidences; everything that happens in our lives has a purpose. The ugly and the cute. Not only is your life on purpose, but it is designed to benefit you. Simply put, it is for your good (**Romans 8:28**). It is not God's desire to bring disaster to your life or to harm you. His plans for you are full of hope and a future (**Jeremiah 29:11**).

This is a hard thing to understand sometimes. Especially when loved ones pass away, jobs are lost, money is tight, and marriages fail. Grief, trauma, and fear are inevitable, but we are called to trust the wisdom of God and not our own understanding. We are called to trust that God can turn even the worst situations into something good. This is His promise to us. Tough times will NOT take you out. They will build character, increase your relationship with Christ, and connect you deeper to the body of Christ. When we call on God, He will answer. When we search for Him in our lives, He will be found (**Jeremiah 29:13**). What a glorious promise! We can trust wholeheartedly that God's plan is perfect, even when we don't understand it. Living a life according to God's plans and purpose for you doesn't mean you won't fail sometimes.

Even as we fail and stumble things are working in our favor.

"And we know that all things work together for good to them that love God, to the who are the called according to his purpose" Romans 8:28 KJV.

How amazing is it to know that God knew us and understood us in advance? Before we knew Christ, He knew us. He chose us. He called us. He gave us right standing with Himself and now we can have a relationship with God. What an amazing and powerful truth. The totality of our purpose is rooted in this fact: We are God's chosen and purposed people. This fact doesn't change, period. No matter how much you struggle with sin, no matter how many times you have had to ask for forgiveness, no matter how many times you keep messing up.

Who you are never changes to God. You still have purpose and power in Christ.

Your past does not define you. Your past does not change your status in the kingdom, kill your witness as a Christian, or remove your virtue as a woman. In fact, on the contrary, your past, your experiences, your struggles, and your pain are what make your story necessary in the kingdom of God. Your testimony is the greatest story you can ever tell. No one can tell your story like you. In God's economy it is more important that we present ourselves authentically rather than presenting ourselves perfectly. That's not true Christianity despite what society says. Acting like a Christian doesn't make you any more Christ like than pretending to be a doctor actually makes you a skilled physician. That's why I read Proverbs 31 and feel utterly unworthy. We are not perfect, but God's plan, purpose, and power has been placed inside our hearts the moment we accepted Him as Lord & savior.

God wants to fulfill His ultimate purpose through YOU. Yes, you have a calling to draw others to Christ. This is the greatest purpose we'll ever have and it can only be accomplished by using the power of God combined with our authentic testimonies.

The greatest access to power that we have is through the name of Jesus:

"Ye have not chosen me, but I have chosen you, and ordained you, that ye should go and bring forth fruit, and that your fruit should remain; that whatsoever ye shall ask of the Father in my name, he may give it to you" John 15:16 KJV.

According to the scriptures, the name of Jesus is a name that is above every name. The name of Jesus will be worshiped by all of creation upon His return. We have been given power through the name of Jesus that can be accessed right now. When we seek God and ask Him to meet our needs according to His will, He will give us whatever we ask for using the name of Jesus.

This is such a powerful statement; but what exactly does it mean? Does it mean that we can ask for any 'ole random thing, or sinful thing, or sexually immoral thing, or prideful thing? Absolutely not! The scripture reassures the purposed and powerful believer that as we live our lives for Christ, as we seek to do His will, whatever we need to accomplish that, He will do for us when we use the name of Jesus. This is a limitless access to power, strength, wisdom, and peace through the powerful name of Jesus.

So why are we suffering emotionally? Why are we walking around without joy, peace, or hope? Is it because we haven't asked God for revival in our hearts? "You have not because you ask not" is a phrase we commonly say. We can trust in the promises of God and rely on Him to provide for our every need in the name of Jesus. This is the power we have in Christ, that we cannot live this life without. God's promises are real, His plans, His purpose, and the power we have through Christ helps us walk out virtue as women of God.

Prayer:

God, Your power is unending and Your love is unfailing. Open up my eyes to see that my strength lies in Your power. You have appointed me and given me the name of Jesus to call out and birth new beginnings in even the driest land. Thank You for choosing me and sustaining me even as I stumble. Help me to live by your power and rebuild my broken places. In Jesus' name, amen.

Highlights:
- You have purpose and power in Christ.
- You can carry and conquer your heavy load in life.
- God has a plan for good in your life.
- Even as you stumble and fail things are working in your favor.
- The name of Jesus gives you access to power.

Power in Action:
Add this daily affirmation to your list:

"I am filled with the Holy Spirit's Power."

When you begin to feel discouraged or defeated, repeat these words to yourself: "The power of Jesus is within me, there is nothing I cannot do."

You're Beautiful

The enemy would like you to believe that your beauty comes from the outside; the way you look; your hair, skin, body shape, and size. So, he makes you feel bad about your outward appearance. He makes you feel insecure, out of place, unworthy, and unwanted. Like clockwork, it steals your joy. You forget what your mother taught you, you forget the Sunday school lessons, you forget the truth.

In middle school, I was such an itty bitty thing. Long legs and not the curvy ones. Flat all the way around, especially in all the areas that count. Not even 100 pounds yet. I was built nothing like my mother who is a #brickhouse in her own right. I longed for the day that I would have boobs. I won't tell you how old I was when I stopped stuffing my bra. Let's just say I was almost embarrassed in high school dance class as my 'stuffing' almost dropped on the floor of the locker room.

In middle school when what seemed like all of the other girls were moving fast and furious into puberty, I was on the slow train. I was definitely not nearly as developed as the other girls my age. I didn't even need a training bra until 9th grade. I was president of the itty bitty titty committee. Did you guys not call it that?! Just us? I know, disgraceful right?

So, of course none of the boys in my grade looked in my direction. I wasn't approached by boys in a romantic way and they made it clear that my body type was not desirable. I was too skinny, too boney, too tiny, too little, and every other adjective their hormone surged minds could come up with. And guess what? I bought into it. Those little prepubescent boys in middle school sold me a cheap lie and I bought it full price, not even on sale. And I love a good sale!

That's the moment when I began rejecting the truth my mama tried to instill in me and I began to look for the approval of others to validate my physical beauty. Now here I am so many years later and I'm still doing the hard inner work of rediscovering where my real beauty lies. Three pregnancies, one C-section, 25lbs, and tons of stretch marks later; I like to think I'm a work in progress. But on my worst days I still hear the voices of disdain for my body; some days the voice is my own. See, these lies run deep and they persist long after the words are said. Ladies, we need to toss out the junk, it's way past its expiration date.

Inner beauty. That's what matters most. No matter how beautiful you think you are on the outside. No matter whether you were praised in school as the best looking girl or talked about until you believed you were on the bottom. When Christ returns He's coming for a church that doesn't have a spot or wrinkle and I'm not talking about foreheads. Looking good is fine, taking care of yourself is necessary, but outward beauty won't help you heal the deep wounds of your past.

How do you think Jesus will be able to tell who's who when He returns? By looking at the heart of all men. As a believer, you have the necessary task of comprehending God's definition of beauty for your own sake. It is crucial that you know just how beautiful you are to God. You are beautiful on both the inside and the outside, but not because of your works. It's because of Jesus' gift of eternal life; our inheritance.

You may know this fact but still rely heavily on your deeds to display your beauty. Your amazing prayers before the church, your inspirational IG posts, blog articles, or service to the community. These are all great actions but they don't make you who you are. And if those works aren't rooted in the truth, then the enemy will try to use them, too, to confuse, distract, and deceive you. Facebook and the comparison trap will have you thinking you are dirt when God has called you much higher. The hard truth is that you are beautiful simply because God declares your beauty through Christ.

Our connection to God and our ability to walk out virtue in our daily lives rests in the truth that God declares you beautiful. When He sees you He sees Jesus Christ. To truly embrace this great fact, kingdom women don't need beauty tips, we need beauty truth!

Beauty Truth #1: God created you in His image and it was Good.

In Genesis 1:27, 31 the Bible says, "So God created human beings in his own image. In the image of God he created them; male and female he created them...Then God looked over all he had made, and he saw that it was very good!"

Beauty was imparted into you the moment God created man. We were created in His image; we acted like Him, walked like Him, thought like Him, and looked like Him; the most beautiful, majestic and holy God. God looked at what He created and declared it GOOD. How amazing it was to be in that moment and receive the ultimate compliment. To be given the greatest honor among creation. To be made in the image of the infinite God who formed the seas and brought forth life at the sound of His voice. We, us, YOU are beautiful beyond measure. This beauty doesn't fade or change because of another person's opinion, even your own.

Beauty Truth #2: When God sees us, He sees Christ, therefore trusting in Christ we can have confidence in who we are, which is good and beautiful.

The sacrifice of Jesus' life on the cross not only secured our place in heaven but it also bridged the gap between an unholy people and a righteous God. That ransom, that redemption is exactly what we can have confidence in as children of God walking out virtue in our everyday lives. *"For God made Christ, who never sinned, to be the offering for our sin, so that we could be made right with God through Christ"* 2 Corinthians 5:21 NLT.

According to Colossians 3:3, "For you died to this life, and your real life is hidden with Christ in God." As we struggle through our individual traumas, challenges, and failures this truth gives us peace. Peace that we are firmly planted in the arms of Jesus even as He helps us get better day by day.

Your position is set, your fate sealed. Not one ounce of insecurity is necessary. We can have complete confidence in the finished work of Jesus Christ on the cross and that what God declared completely and utterly beautiful on day one, is equally beautiful today: simply because of Christ.

Beauty Truth #3: No amount of sin can change your worth in Christ.

How about that? Go back and reread it, sis. All the lies the enemy has been throwing at you all your life are just that: LIES. Let this truth sink into the core of your being. Let it enter into your ears, penetrate your heart, and infiltrate your mind. Let this truth of God transform, renew, and elevate your thinking. Seeping past head knowledge and developing into deep understanding. Luke 12:6-7 says, "What is the price of five sparrows—two copper coins? Yet God does not forget a single one of them. And the very hairs on your head are all numbered. So don't be afraid; you are more valuable to God than a whole flock of sparrows."

You are valued by God. You mean so much more to God than even the birds in the air and no amount of struggle with sin will change that. God is not challenged by your struggles, He is ready to meet you where you are. He deeply knows and understands that we are tempted by sin and He is more than able to do something about it **(1 Corinthians 10:13)**.

Beauty Truth #4: Real beauty shines from the inside out

They say beauty is in the eyes of the beholder. Well, no statement could be more true than this as it relates to your beauty in Christ. The Bible specifically and intentionally differentiates between false beauty and true beauty. God urges His people to not be concerned with the way things look on the outside but to rather examine the heart.

"But the Lord said unto Samuel, Look not on his countenance, or on the height of his stature; because I have refused him: for the Lord teeth not as a man teeth; for man looking on the outward appearance, but the Lord looketh at the heart." 1 Samuel 16:7 KJV.

The world judges by the outward appearance and is often deceived. Your mother probably told you as a child not to judge a book by its cover; and for good reason. You simply can't tell what something is until you open it up and take a look on the inside.

Ironically, I've seen this same principle come alive in my dating life through the years. As cute as I think I am (hehe), I have never been known as the hottest girl in the room. I am often overlooked and underestimated at first. I can't tell you how many times I've heard "wow, I didn't realize you were so amazing" only after seeing me for a while then getting to know me. You'd think I would be flattered but my inner annoyed girl just rolls her eyes and feels judged. What was really said is "I didn't take the time to properly notice you, but when I did I saw your real beauty." Again, not flattered at all. What I desire, what I think all women desire, is to be seen for my natural beauty; it may not stop traffic but it definitely exudes true beauty. No one wants to be noticed as an afterthought, it's not a fair judgement.

Thank God for Jesus who is nothing like us. Inside of a (wo)man's heart is where you'll find the truth of who she is, not the outside. God has placed a real, true beauty on the inside of you that flows from the inside out.

"Whose adorning let it not be that outward adorning of plaiting the hair, and of wearing of gold, or of putting on apparel; but let it be the hidden man of the heart, in that which is not corruptible, even the ornament of a meek and quiet spirit, which is in the sight of God of great price" 1 Peter 3:3-4 KJV.

Isn't it funny that the same character traits that the world deems as below standard are the same traits of femininity, gentleness, and strength that God says possess the greatest value of beauty in His kingdom? As women we are always trying to look beautiful, to be pleasing to the opposite sex, to feel good when we look in the mirror.

Are the things we desire to be seen as beautiful a twisted version of a better form of beauty ordained by God? Absolutely! Wouldn't you rather have a true beauty that doesn't fade with age, gravity, or subjectivity? I know I would. Thankfully, Jesus offers us so much more than mere short-lived beauty. No amount of subjectivity can change that. He offers us eternal life and true beauty in Christ.

Simply put: We have been lied to. We have been deceived. We have allowed the tricks of the enemy to become more real in our lives than the powerful truth of scripture. We have failed to truly insert these biblical truths into our system and have suffered tremendously because of it. You are not alone, I'm talking to myself.

But we still have an opportunity.

God, being rich in mercy has given us yet another chance to embrace His truth and reject the enemy's lies about ourselves. When we know who we are, it not only affects us personally, but it will impact the lives of those around us, too. You are not being selfish for learning about who you are in Christ, you do not lack any humility because you seek to understand how God feels about you. When Jesus ascended into heaven, He left us with these truths because it is TRUTH that will set us free (**John 8:32**). Not our feelings, not a smaller waistline, not our experiences, not our goals or aspirations, but the truth of God.

Listen, I know your thighs rub too close, your belly hangs over your pants, and your bum has dimples all over it. Guess what, mine does, too; but praise God that He does not judge by outward appearance. The value that He's placed on your life has nothing to do with the terrible things that have been spoken over you. So reject the lies with me. Put down the deeply rooted voices that say you are not worthy of love. Listen to the still, small voice of the Holy Spirit as He whispers, "You are beautiful, my child."

Now take a minute and pause. Take a deep breath in for 5 seconds, hold it for 5 seconds, and then release it for 5 seconds. As you do this, breathe in the new view of yourself, the one established by God before the foundations of the Earth. Hold your breath and feel the power of God consume your heart, change your mind, and establish your thoughts. Then finally exhale your breath and release every negative thought, action, or deed that says the opposite of what God has already called truth.

Now rest in the truth, beloved. You are a beautiful representation of God's grace & love.

Prayer:

God, I praise You because Your word never returns void. You have called me beautiful. Help me to feel that truth deep in my heart. May it fill every void left behind by those who did not understand who I am. Thank You for seeing value in me and cherishing me by the power of Jesus' work on the cross. In Jesus' name, amen.

Highlights:
- Inner beauty is what matters most.
- Your beauty doesn't rely on your works or outward appearance.
- You were created in the image of God and it was good.
- When God sees you, He sees Christ. Trusting in Christ we can have confidence in who we are, which is a good and beautiful creation.
- No struggle with sin can change your value in Christ.

- Your real beauty shines from the inside out. Go ahead and let your light shine.

Beauty in Action:
- Get a piece of paper, start a list, "I would be more beautiful if..."
- Make this list as long as you have ideas. Include everything that you think will make you beautiful.
- Now tear it up.
- Say the BEAUTIFUL prayer over the broken pieces of paper:

B God help me to *BELIEVE* that I am beautiful because you call me beautiful.

E Give me *EYES* to see what true beauty is.

A I *APPRECIATE* the sacrifice Jesus made on the cross just for me.

U *UNDO* all the past pain and trauma that keeps me bound to unhealthy thought patterns.

T *TEACH* me to have confidence in you and not my works.

I Help me to see my IMPERFECTION as a symbol of your work in my life.

F Replace my *FAULTY* thinking with your wisdom.

U *USE* my insecurities to motivate my growth.

L Help me to lay aside the *LIES* I have believed about myself from others.

Irreplaceable

For the last 12 years I've had the privilege of being a mom. The role of mother is a different one. Whether you're the mama to a cute fur-baby or raging toddler; you are the go-to gal for all things lost & found, hunger, aches and pains. Mothers are referees, tutors, chefs, maids, entertainers, lawyers, doctors, and spiritual advisors. It's amazing just how much your children need you. I grew up in a single parent home as the youngest of three girls. Ironically, my blessing has also been being the mom of 3 amazing little girls similarly to the way I grew up. When I say some of my days feel like deja-vu, please believe me. I'm living in the twilight zone! My children's personalities resemble those of my siblings. (Enter unresolved birth order conflicts.) Y'all, I'm raising a mini version of my sisters, their dad, and me all in one household.

These girls have stretched my patience and my love. I am truly learning what it really means to be a parent, a caregiver, and a provider. Sometimes cruising, sometimes stumbling, but learning nonetheless. To have these little people looking up to you for everything at all times. To be responsible for imparting wisdom and truth to them; it's such a blessed and necessary challenge. Key emphasis on the challenge part.

My two older daughters, better known as Am-Bam and Han-Han, are only two years apart so, of course they tend to fight and argue the most. I'm often caught in the middle of a disagreement. They have opposite personalities but work very well together when they learn to accept their differences. But of course, like most opposite personality pairs it's a whole lot easier said than done.

I remember one disagreement in particular that really affected Han-Han. You know, one of those moments where the only solution involved Mama becoming the judge and jury. Han-Han wanted something from her sister and went about it the wrong way. If you know Han-Han this is not out of her character. She is my most low key, laid back, chill child; until you push her buttons.

Well, let's just say the judge didn't rule in Han-Han's favor this time. After my judgement, Han-Han, my special middle child, told me that I didn't like her. She felt that I liked Am-Bam more because of the decision I made. It struck me hard at first and made me question my own motives. It's hard looking in the face of your child who's in pain. I could tell she was really hurt, but what was her pain rooted in? Truth? Lies? Was I really being partial to one child and not the other? Is it even possible for me to give special treatment to either one? I reflected internally a bit before responding to her comment. I've learned that in those short reflective moments the Holy Spirit has a way illuminating a situation. Praise God because these children stump me daily. Like a light bulb in that moment, even as I questioned my own self, the truth of God was made clear to me.

The way I treat each of my children will never be equal, but it will always be fair and just. Each one of my children are very special with their own unique desires and challenges. Not ONE of them is replaceable. I will give consequences and rewards to each of them according to their individual circumstances. I explained this to her in words she could understand. I wanted her to really GET IT. I wanted her to comprehend that more than wanting the equal treatment (or the things) her sister gets, I want my daughter to know that SHE is special and what's for her is exclusively for her. Even her punishments that feel so very bad at the time are all designed for her good. No need to compare, feel less than, left out, or jealous. Why? Because God says so. His truth trumps all lies and He calls us all His chosen. God created you special and irreplaceable and there's no one or nothing that can change that truth.

God calls you His masterpiece.

"For we are God's masterpiece. He has created us anew in Christ Jesus, so we can do the good things he planned for us long ago" Ephesians 2:10 NLT.

Has anyone ever called you inadequate, ugly, lazy, unworthy, basic, or ordinary? Well, guess what? They lied! You, my dear, are so far from those derogatory names. You are a masterpiece. God created you with perfection in mind. You were formed in your mother's womb as the epitome of God's creation; a being in the image of God. No lie from any person in this world can change that. You are no afterthought, no accident, no oopsy to God: you are a masterpiece meant to do good things in Christ.

Isaiah 43:4 tells us that "others were given in exchange for you. I traded their lives for yours because you are precious to me. You are honored, and I love you." You are fully wanted by God. Even through your broken family, your single parent home, your regretful abortion, the abuse you suffered, the adoption you don't speak about; God still calls you special. You are precious to God and not easily replaced as the world tries to convince you. No matter what they see, God sees you as His masterpiece.

You have been chosen by God.

Do you remember playing dodgeball or kickball in elementary school? For some this time in recess was where the fun began but for others, including me, it was a sad time. The captain always had their choice of teammates and the official process of picking teams was one that brought about anxiety for me. Most of the time I wasn't chosen first or second. As a super skinny, non-athletic, slow to average runner I was no first draft pick. In fact, unless my closest girlfriend had been randomly chosen as a captain, I could be sure that I would be chosen dead last. Way to boost my self-esteem & reinforce the lies I already believed. In the fifth grade, being chosen last for a game really isn't being chosen at all. It's like they have to take you. No one wants to be "chosen" like that.

According to 1 Peter 2:9, "You are a chosen people. You are royal priests, a holy nation, God's very own possession. As a result, you can show others the goodness of God, for he called you out of the darkness into his wonderful light." We have been chosen and it's nothing like that kickball game in the 5th grade. We are not chosen last, but first. Through Christ, God calls us out of darkness and into relationship with Him.

According to Ephesians 1:4-5, not only did God adopt us into His family, but He decided to do this before the world was made.

"Even before he made the world, God loved us and chose us in Christ to be holy and without fault in his eyes. God decided in advance to adopt us into his own family by bringing us to himself through Jesus Christ. This is what he wanted to do, and it gave him great pleasure" Ephesians 1:4-5 NLT.

Do you understand what this means? God was fully aware of what He was creating. He knew without a shadow of a doubt that His chosen, masterpiece creation, made in his own image, would one day sin. He knew that sin would bring separation and ruin our relationship. Yet, He STILL created us and devised a plan that would allow us to be reconnected to Him through Christ. Now that's amazing. It's so amazing that even on my best day as a mom I would never give my kids an amazing reward knowing full well they wouldn't do right by it. I'm clearly not Jesus, but thank God that we serve a gracious and merciful God.

This sentiment is not something to take lightly. God's advance thought of our adoption, plus His foreknowledge of our fall in the garden, plus His great plan of salvation and His undivided love through Jesus is the greatest equation. It's everything all in one: addition, multiplication, subtraction, and division. It's the ultimate comeback story, the best kind of redemption and we get to be a part of that. God's special and irreplaceable people.

You have a significant place in the body of Christ:

Ever wonder the purpose behind all your kinks and quirky ways? Ever question your existence because you were just a tad bit different than everyone else? This is no accident. God created you this way, but it's not so you can feel like an outsider. Quite the opposite is actually true. You have been uniquely designed by a great architect, made special and exclusively to be united with the body of Christ.

"The church", "The Body of Christ", "Believers", "Saints", "Crazy Jesus freaks"; however you want to call it. This is the united group of all people; past, present, and future who believe in Jesus Christ as Lord and Savior. We are the church, not the building, and Jesus is coming back for us. But before He gets back, He has some pretty spectacular plans that He wishes for the body of Christ to be a part of. We are made unique because it takes a unique set of skills, personalities, interests, characteristics, colors, shapes, and sizes to reach the world for Jesus. Thankfully, you and I have a significant role to play in the amazing body of Christ.

"But now hath God set the members every one of them in the body, as it hath pleased him. And if they were all one member, where were the body? But now are they many members, yet but one body. And the eye cannot say unto the hand, I have no need of thee: nor again the head to the feet, I have no need of you. Nay, much more those members of the body, which seem to be more feeble, are necessary: and those members of the body, which we think to be less honorable, upon these we bestow more abundant honor; and our uncomely parts have more abundant comeliness. For our comely parts have no need: but God hath tempered the body together, having given more abundant honor to that part which lacked: that there should be no schism in the body; but that the members should have the same care for one another. And whether one member suffer, all the members suffer with it; or one member be honoured, all members rejoice with it" 1 Corinthians 12:18-26 KJV.

You have a place, you have a purpose. As a member of Christ's body, you are needed. If you are not in place and operating in your unique gifts given by God, the body is lacking. As believers we are to be salt & light (Matthew 5:13-16). This means we provide flavor by being sprinkled throughout the world. The place that you are right now is exactly where you need to be. We are also to be examples of light by living a Spirit-led life while pointing others to Christ. This design is not by chance, it is the miraculous plan of God. And He wants us to participate in it.

I learned this valuable principle in college. By the grace of God I was able to be a part of the creation of a group of young believers at my university in Saint Louis, MO. We called ourselves Tru Impact because we were making a true impact on our lives, on our campus, and our community. This group of friends and I were miraculously experiencing a spiritual transformation within our hearts at the same time. When I think back over those years, there's no real way to describe the experience of being completely on fire for the Lord, surrounded by other young people who felt the same. Did we experience persecution? Absolutely. Did our peers call us crazy? Yep, they sure did. But the change that God was doing in the hearts of my peers was undeniable. It was nothing short of a revival. A miracle even and God graciously allowed me to be a part of it.

We would have meetings where we would praise & worship God, read and discuss scripture, and have testimony time. Testimony time was the heart of the night. It was the best part about the meeting and you never knew what would happen. God would send people who had heard about us from all over St. Louis; they prayed for us, prophesied over us, and gave us an encouraging word. Lots of people came through these meetings, some we never knew, some would become lifelong friends, and some we would never see again. They were all sent by God and we knew that.

During one Tru Impact meeting, right in the middle of testimony time, a young black male entered the room. At this time the room we met in was in the already busy epicenter of the university, the student center. Students from all over the city were packed wall-to-wall in this room. The young man came into the standing room only space and stood there for a while, just taking in the atmosphere. When an opportunity came for him to speak he began to tell us his story.

This young man worked at our school in the culinary department and got off of work around 9pm. As he began to speak slowly with a tremble in his voice, he talked about his struggles with money, his past history of violence & crime, and how he had been trying to do the right thing, but it was getting too hard. He went on to say that he felt so down about his situation and the lack of improvement that he planned to rob someone for money that very night once he got off work.

But just as he got ready to leave his workstation that night, he heard singing, he heard praising, and he saw young people pouring into this room; our room. He walked towards the commotion and came in. He told us that as he came into the room, his heart was touched and he was convicted by the Holy Spirit. He confessed his plan of robbery to us and asked for prayer. Then he made a decision to turn his life over to Christ and be saved. We prayed with this man, sung praises to God for this man, exchanged contact information, and then he left and we never saw him again.

That night I learned a very valuable lesson. God puts us in the right place at the right time for salvation to be reached by all who desire. All we have to do is trust Him, trust our place in the body of Christ, trust His plan and our purpose found in Him. If we were not there that night, someone may have gotten robbed, maybe even one of us. That man may have jeopardized his life and an opportunity to submit to Christ. But because of our merciful God we were there, Jesus put us there to make a true impact, just as our group name stated. You are incredibly special to God and irreplaceable in His plan. He will use you to bring about salvation to the entire world. We are not worthy, yet He chooses us daily. What a glorious God we serve!

Prayer:

Lord, I thank You that I am more than just a fleeting thought or a speck of dust in Your eyes. God, You chose me to have a relationship and I do not take that lightly. Help me to walk as a chosen, bent but not broken, masterpiece of Your creation. Lord, I want to rest in Your words, I want to rest in this truth. In Jesus' name, amen.

Highlights:

- God calls you His masterpiece.
- You are precious to God and not easily replaced.
- You have been chosen and you have a purpose.
- Your individuality has a special place in the body of Christ.
- If you are not in place and operating in your unique gifts given by God, the body is lacking.

Purpose in Action:

- Reflect in your journal about the following questions, then pray asking God for what you need.
- What are you most passionate about?
- How does your passion serve others?
- What is unique about the way you address this passion?
- What do you need from God to continue to walk out this passion in your life?

Forgiven Me

Summer break is a rough time for this mama. Homeschooling has been a huge part of our journey as a family for four years. I've learned to balance both being a stay at home mom and a working mom all while being responsible for my children's academic success. On one hand, because of the work I do, I have been blessed to spend most of the summer with my kids for the past several years. On the other hand, because of the work I do, I am blessed to be driven crazy for 3 months straight by my kids. No, really it is a blessing. I know that and I really appreciate it, but the challenges are REAL. Now don't get me wrong, our daily schedule as a homeschool family can be stressful, but it's managed stress. It's planned and it's structured. Yes, they are home but it's still school. So when breaks come around we BREAK.

Most summer breaks start off really good. I create a schedule, plan some activities, some moments of rest, work time, outdoor exploration; blah, blah, blah. It all sounds good on paper until my 3 sweet little girls turn into undefeated, heavyweight boxing champions of the world. Not even a few days into summer break, like clockwork, they start fighting.

Oh, how I wish they would limit it to just arguing but these little ladies get physical, too. I jokingly say they get it from their dad's side because my sisters and I were never physical. My girls love wrestling, sparing on the hardwood floor, and throwing unexpected jabs.

The fighting seems to never end. Day in and day out it's, 'I hate you but I love you and can't stop playing with you' petty sibling rivalry. Next thing I know Mama is frustrated and there goes the schedule, all the activities, and any hope of fun that I had. I really put some thought into those schedules! I googled all the fun places to visit. We were actually going to be cultured & exquisite. Or at least that's what it looked like in my dreams.

I've developed a bit of trauma because of this repetitive habit we cycle through every school break. So even throughout the year, as we hit winter break, spring break, or any other day off, I immediately get nervous and frustrated about the anticipated fighting. I find myself preparing for an all out brawl that hasn't even happened yet. Trauma, worry, and anxiety kick in because I remember the last break. Once it's over I tend to just leave it where it was. I don't pray about it afterwards and I definitely don't completely surrender this issue to God. I walk away, bury it with all the other issues, and then start all over again with the next new challenge. Which basically means I'm still trying to fix it on my own. What's worse is that the feelings begin to resurface as the days pass and shame sets in. I feel ashamed because IT happened again. I feel like a terrible mom and an even worse example of a Christian woman.

All of this has a direct impact on the way I treat my kids. When I'm stressed all grace goes out of the window. Amazing grace? Ummm no, more like get out of my face. I'm short with my words, inconsiderate of their concerns, and an overall a grumpy mom. I haven't walked out forgiveness for them or myself properly since the last break. It's no wonder that same issue keeps repeating itself. Every time they're out of school I freak out because I remember the past, I remind them of it, and I internally expect them to do the same bad things again.

Friends, I welcomed a vicious cycle of parenting unforgiveness in my heart. I create a situation by expecting my unrealistic dreams of summer break to be a reality, then I try to fix it by ignoring it. Then I look for my children to do better the next time without actually doing the work it takes to set them up for success. This cycle births bitterness in my heart, perpetuates the comparison trap and breeds negativity in the household. Unforgiveness is contagious and latches on to those closest to you. Forgiveness isn't just about those who offend you, it's often about recognizing who you offend, even in parenting, and how to reconcile those situations so they don't fester into greater wounds.

Relief is what I feel knowing God is nothing like me. When I'm in the depths of internal deception after I've believed the enemy's lies about my family, I've accepted unforgiveness and bitterness instead of peace and reconciliation. Why couldn't I see how much I needed God more than a summer plan? How could I be so annoyed by my own children that I prayed for God to bring into my life that I only expected the worst from them? What made me think that I should expect forgiveness and grace from God when I wasn't willing to do the same for myself and my girls?

"Instead, be kind to each other, tenderhearted, forgiving one another, just as God through Christ has forgiven you" Ephesians 4:32 NLT.

Receiving God's forgiveness in our own lives should cause us to act differently. A person whose many sins are forgiven can't help but to love much **(Luke 7:47)**. Do your actions towards the world around you illustrate God's forgiveness in your life? Are you letting your own forgiveness come from a place of plenty or scarcity? You have been abundantly forgiven. Sis, it's the most important truth you need to know today. Not kinda forgiven like what I've done with my kids before; where God expects us to keep doing wrong and treats us like our past sins are fresh on His mind. No, that's not how God forgives us. He forgives us wholly and completely; we are forgiven today, tomorrow, and forever.

Christ's finished work on the cross covers all your past, present, and future sins. No matter what has happened or when; if we confess our sins, repent, and turn from our wicked ways we are forever forgiven by a God who even knows that you'll do it again. In order to walk in forgiveness and be the virtuous woman of God that you are, you must truly understand what it means to be forgiven. We must also know exactly how God handles our repentant sins. We know we are forgiven but why and how? How does God do it, how can we be assured that our past sins do not shame, haunt, or persecute us any longer?

What happens when God forgives us?

Your record is cleared & your sins are put out of God's sight:

"Blessed is he whose transgression is forgiven, Whose sin is covered. Blessed is the man unto whom the Lord imputeth not iniquity, and in whose spirit there is no guile" Psalm 32: 1-2 KJV.

I'll never forget the day the judge discharged my debt from bankruptcy. At the time I was a new wife and mother with thousands of dollars in student loans, I was underemployed and stressed out. I saw this process as my only way to get out of the immense financial pressure that I was experiencing. Sure I was nervous about rebuilding my credit and the negative impact it would have on my future goals. But given my other options, I chose to see bankruptcy as a beneficial tool.

I was overjoyed, to say the least. Not because I had frivolously created debt that I no longer owed and was ready to start that cat and mouse game all over again. Nope. I was filled with gratitude as I realized how much hope my future offered having gone through such a tough financial lesson. I was given a chance that many do not get: a chance to start over with a clean slate. Those debts that once kept me up at night were now only a memory. No more debt collectors calling or anxiety keeping me stuck. I felt free. Bank account was still on E...but I was free.

Friends, this is how we can feel knowing that God has forgiven our sins. Your slate has been cleared and God no longer identifies you by your sin. With repentance comes forgiveness. This is God's order and there's nothing you can do about it except be filled with the joy of knowing that the dirt you did doesn't keep you dirty. God literally removes it from His sight.

In addition to moving your sins out of His sight;

God removes your sins out of His mind:

"And I will forgive their wickedness, and I will never again remember their sins" Jeremiah 31:34b NLT.

What the what? Out of His mind, you say? Absolutely! The idea that God will actually cease to remember my sins blows my mind. Insert mind-blow emoji! I know God to be a lot of amazing things. One of His attributes that I am in constant awe of is His Omniscience. God is omniscient; this simply means He is all-knowing. He knows the intentions of every person's heart, He knows the past and the future, He knows what you and I will do before we even think to do it. Talk about being intimately known and seen.

The God of the universe CHOOSES to remove our sin from His mind...for our sake. I can't stress enough how mind-boggling this is. God cannot lie. God is unable to be unjust or unfair or create a reality that isn't real. Unlike our nature that is drawn to deceit, being in denial is not an option for God. He is Holy. What difference does this make? Let me make it clear. We are not forgiven because God has ignored our guilt; He doesn't pretend it didn't happen. Nope. Jesus' death on the cross, His resurrection, and His defeat over sin satisfies our sin debt and replaces our punishment. Jesus paid the price **(Romans 6:23)**. So when God removes your sin out of His mind it is a Just, Righteous, and Holy thing to do. Our debt is paid in FULL.

It's similar to how my bankruptcy got the debt monkey off my back (at least temporarily until I made more debt). Except Jesus' work is eternal. I don't have to go back for a second, third, or fourth round of salvation. I can humbly and directly ask for forgiveness and trust that my slate is cleared by a perfect God. Cue the shouting music and the confetti. God has miraculously removed your sin; the dirtiest of sin is far from His mind.

Your sins are out of God's reach:

"He has removed our sins as far from us as the east is from the west" Psalm 103:12 NLT.

"Once again you will have compassion on us. You will trample our sins under your feet and throw them into the depths of the ocean!" Micah 7:19 NLT.

Can I be real for a minute? There are some things, people, and places I'd like to forget I've ever been to or associated with. Even worse, there are other people, still alive might I add, who know where I've been and what I did. Words said that can't be undone, terrible thoughts, evil and vindictive plans personally crafted by yours truly. The self-proclaimed recovering perfectionist. Yikes! Sometimes it feels like the past can haunt you.

The good news is, this isn't the case with God. He doesn't condemn us. In fact, He puts our sins completely out of our reach; "-as far as the east is from the west". If you feel condemnation about the sins you've repented for, girl that isn't Jesus, that's the devil. *"So now there is no condemnation for those who belong to Christ Jesus"* Romans 8:1 NLT.

God knows that sin stifles, distracts, discourages, and limits our growth as believers. So when He forgives us, His will isn't that it lingers over our heads or haunts us like an old ex-boyfriend. God knows it has to be out of our reach in order for us to truly arrive at our fullest potential in Christ. But honey, if you don't know this truth or more importantly if you don't believe this truth, the enemy will steal your peace.

See, it's the compassion for me! We serve a God of limitless compassion. He feels our pain, He knows our struggles, He is not far from our challenges, and He is ready and willing to meet our needs. That is what moves God to figuratively toss our mess and junk into the sea. There is no one else that loves you as passionately as Jesus does. There is no one else that will move on your behalf giving you exactly what you need to be free. Our king Jesus has done this; now you and I must walk in this truth. Believe it. Hold on to it. Even when the waves of shame are trying to take us under.

Your sins no longer exist.

"I—yes, I alone—will blot out your sins for my own sake and will never think of them again" Isaiah 43:25 NLT.

"I have swept away your sins like a cloud. I have scattered your offenses like the morning mist" Isaiah 44:22a NLT.

Long gone are the late night college partying days when you wake up feeling dazed and confused yet with a hint of delight. No real stress, no real bills, no real responsibilities. Hello 30+, fatigue, back pain, and adulting woes. Have you ever been sitting by yourself with your own thoughts and emotions and said "my life isn't supposed to be this way?" Yep, me too! We feel like this because it's true. Each stage of our lives takes us to a brand new set of struggles, pain points, and pressures. So although I no longer (on most days) wake up dazed and confused and my life now mostly brings me daily #momlife struggles, God's desire is that I wake up unbothered by my former sins because they no longer exist to Him.

God blots out our sin. But not like I try to blot out a stain in my spill-riden, well worn carpet. When God blots out our sins it's as if they never existed. Move over Dyson & Shark; let the big man upstairs teach you how it's done. Girl, God isn't sitting on the throne with a list of all your wrongs, adding to it with each move you make. He's your coach, He's your encourager, He's your stain remover!

Have you ever looked up at the sky in awe of how it moves? I love nature. Well, let me be clear. I've grown to love nature. My favorite thing to do in nature is simply to watch it. I love watching the way waves move in the ocean or the way the wind moves and blows. Nature watching is just about as entertaining for me as people watching, which I love, too. But I digress.

Watching the clouds in the sky; picking out the symbols and shapes I see especially from an airplane is mesmerizing. Clouds move so fast sometimes. You see one, then in the blink of an eye, it's gone. Something that you just had eyes on, something that moved you to stop and stare, almost disappears as it passes in the sky. Sis, this is our sin to God. Removed. Gone. Poof. It simply no longer exists. But can you believe it? Will you receive this truth? Can you allow God's truth to change the way you see yourself and others?

Your Conscience Cleansed.

"How much more shall the blood of Christ, who through the eternal Spirit offered himself without spot to God, purge your conscience from dead works to serving the living God?" Hebrews 9:14 KJV.

"Let us draw near with a true heart in full assurance of faith, having our hearts sprinkled from an evil conscience, and our bodies washed with pure water" Hebrews 10:22 KJV.

Can I pause and give you a virtual high-five? If you've made it this far into the longest, most repetitive chapter of this book, it's safe to say that you are fighting to get this truth. I'm right there with you. I commend you, I honor your desire, and I salute your persistence. The lies we've believed for a long time didn't get into our brains over night and the truth that sets us free has to be heard again and again **(Romans 10:17).**

I am forgiven and God says I no longer have a guilty conscience about it. This is the truth I've struggled with the most. If you're anything like me a guilty conscience has held you back from so many things. Feeling guilty or ashamed can keep you stuck, bound to fear, and paralyzed. If you are unable to walk in the freedom God has so graciously given you, then you definitely can't do what He is calling you to do. You definitely can't start over, begin again, pivot, or any other adjective I can think of that means to truly change.

These two very powerful previous scriptures teach us one of the greatest lessons about who God is.   Once our sins are forgiven a relationship with God is restored. This is huge! Don't miss this. The primary goal for even sending Jesus to the cross, for allowing us an opportunity to repent and be forgiven, is to establish a true relationship with God the father. True relationships are always the goal. God isn't interested in robots; He's interested in relationships. God wants us to worship Him in Spirit and in Truth (John 4:24). God wants us to be in His presence.

Sin separates us from God; Jesus' work on the cross and our subsequent forgiveness restores us into a "right-standing" relationship with God. Friends, we no longer have to be ashamed about all the things we've done. We no longer have to be afraid. We no longer have an enemy, we now have a savior and friend in God.

There is a place for Godly sorrow and repentance. Guilt of wrongdoing should bring you to the foot of the cross, but friends, we don't arrive at the foot of the cross uncertain of what God will do. We go with security and blessed assurance knowing that He will forgive us and clear our conscience, allowing us to have a renewed relationship with Him. God is a God of restoration, security, compassion, and grace. You can trust, no matter what you've done, that your sin and your conscience has been made clean by the blood of Jesus.

Am I beating a dead horse here? Well, I should hope so! This is one of the most important truths of them all. I think I've said that about each one. Well, guess what? I'm right each time. This is the foundation of your freedom. When you accepted the Lord Jesus as your savior it began with repentance and the forgiveness of your sins. The enemy will attempt to attack you in this area every chance he gets. Knowing without a shadow of doubt who God is and what He has and IS still doing for you is the game changer here.

Who can shake you when you know the truth? What lie can deter you when you know the truth? What scheme can take you off course when you know the truth? What sin can separate you from God when you know the truth?

"For I am persuaded, that neither death, nor life, nor angels, nor principalities, nor powers, nor things present, nor things to come, nor height, nor depth, more any other creature, shall be able to separate us from the love of God, which is in Christ Jesus our Lord" Romans 8: 38-39 KJV.

Ladies, this counts for the new messy things you will do in the future, too. You know, the housewives style drama; the gossip we all crave and every non-productive thing we end up doing except drinking our water and minding our own business. If you have children, even "good behaving" ones make poor choices. It doesn't matter if you've been walking with Christ for 10 minutes or 10 years; all of the sin you have or will do is covered by the blood of Jesus. No, we don't have a sin pass that allows us to act out, go off, and abuse the Grace of God **(Romans 6:15-18).**

Absolutely not! What we have is a Daddy, an Abba, who loves us dearly. He is near to us, He cares for us, He wants good for us; and when we need discipline He lovingly gives it to us. Albeit kicking and screaming most days. But make no mistake here, although we are adequately disciplined as His children, we are also abundantly forgiven.

In our appreciation and gratitude for this great Grace, we are moved to do righteous works that bring honor and glory to God's name. We can now be the virtuous women of God that we are, simply because we understand that nothing holds us back. No sin, no shame, no condemnation is powerful enough to negate the fact that God forgives us eternally.

"You, dear children, are from God and have overcome them, because the one who is in you is greater than the one who is in the world" 1 John 4:4 NLT.

Prayer:
Heavenly Father, my mind cannot understand how You forgive, but God I thank You anyway. Your forgiveness fuels the very air that I breathe. Help me today to feel forgiven like I've learned that I am. Help me to embrace Your forgiveness that doesn't change or can be taken from me. Thank You for Jesus' sacrifice on the cross and for the many sins You have already forgiven in my life. As I accept Your forgiveness, Lord help me to live out forgiveness to those around me. In Jesus' name, amen.

Highlights:
- Receiving God's forgiveness in our own lives should cause us to act differently.
- When God forgives, your record is cleared & your sins are put out of God's sight. **(Psalm 32:1-2)**
- God removes your sins out of His mind. **(Jeremiah 31:34b)**
- Your sins are out of God's reach. **(Psalm 103:12)**

- Your sins no longer exist. **(Isaiah 43:25)**
- Your conscience is cleansed. **(Hebrews 10:22)**
- A true relationship with God is always the goal. God isn't interested in robots; He's interested in relationships.

Forgiveness in Action:

- Make a decision to forgive today. It doesn't matter who or what it is, but let this be a personal act of surrender and thanksgiving. Surrender, because you acknowledge God's plan to use forgiveness to bring about His love. Thanksgiving, because you acknowledge the gravity of the forgiveness you have received by the Father.
- Forgiveness is an action word. You may not feel ready but trust God to give you what you need as you take baby steps towards forgiveness daily.

Warrior

Eight

Y ou've heard about who God is to you. You realize how loved, chosen, cherished, and eternally forgiven you are. By now you know exactly how big of a price was paid for your place in the kingdom of God. You know you have a purpose and you can feel it stirring in your very soul. So what now? Well, my friend...now you learn to fight.

I know I complained earlier about my kids fighting. It really is hard for me to watch. Most of the time they are just playing but 'play' doesn't register with me like that. Someone told me once, just let them fight it out. So I did and ironically it worked out. They would fight and work it out themselves. Almost like the physical energy needed to be released. I still don't get it but they've taught me a valuable lesson that I want to share with you.

There is a time for fighting.

Fight? You're probably thinking what is this crazy lady talking about, this book is not supposed to be about fighting. Lean in for a bit, my beloved: if you don't learn to fight the small battles you can't enjoy the success of the big win. Sis, you're a winner! The reason why you're a winner is because God birthed a mighty warrior inside of you. Yes, you! You are a mighty warrior of God. Equipped with the truth and armed for battle, you can knock down every scheme and trick the enemy throws your way. No matter how deep the wound may be you can have the victory in Christ.

Let's face it, we live in the midst of warfare. Not necessarily a physical battle, although this may be true depending on where you live. We walk around everyday in the middle of spiritual warfare.

"For we wrestle not against flesh and blood, but against principalities, against powers, against the rulers of the darkness of this world, against spiritual wickedness in high places" Ephesians 6:12 KJV.

The struggles you and I have, the people who rub us the wrong way, the issue in your marriage, the rift between friends, the disagreements among family; these are all examples of spiritual battles that take place every day. Without looking at these situations from spiritual eyes you'd be moved to only find a tangible solution such as conflict resolution or counseling. There is nothing wrong with tangible solutions but according to the scripture above there is a fight taking place in heavenly places that affects what happens in the physical world around us. Last time I checked, tangible solutions do nothing in the spirit realm.

So let's make this clear. First, we have very real spiritual battles, things in the unseen spiritual world that affect us in the physical world every day. Second, we have the ability to affect this unseen world and the spiritual battles that take place within it which thereby helps the physical world we experience daily **(Matthew 18:18).** Are you following me? Good. This leads me to my big point:

Sis, we gotta fight!

I don't know if you're like me and have damsel in distress syndrome, knight in shining armor disease, or the save me flu but let me be the first to tell you these conditions do not exempt you from bearing your own cross, working out your own salvation, conquering your giants, and overcoming your fears. You are a warrior! A warrior princess if you must, but still a mighty and powerful warrior of God. Jesus has saved you and equipped you for every battle by the power of the Holy Spirit; you don't need confirmation of your abilities from anyone else. You do however need the right weapons.

"Wherefore take unto you the whole armor of God, that yet may be able to withstand in the evil day, and having done all, to stand. Stand therefore, having your loins girt about with truth, and having on the breastplate of righteousness; and your feet shod with the preparation of the gospel of peace; above all, taking the shield of faith, wherewith yet shall be able to quench all the fiery arts of the wicked. And take the helmet of salvation, and the sword of the Spirit, which is the word of God" Ephesians 6:13-17 KJV.

I am not a fighter. Obviously you know that by now as you've read how the shock and awe of my pritsy girls fighting sends me into a mental breakdown. I'm sure all the #boymoms are giving me the side eye right about now. However, those that have been on the receiving end of one of my tongue lashings would say otherwise. (Pray for me. God is definitely not done with me yet.) The point is I am not a physical fighter. I didn't grow up getting into fights, I didn't physically fight my siblings or kids in school, or get involved in neighborhood brawls (Hey, it was the 90's #thuglife). I preferred to get along with others and still do. I've always recognized that not everyone will like you or get along with you but I am more likely to make friends and not enemies in a new space. It's a weird mix of maturity and people pleasing, if I'm honest.

Now, this isn't to say I never have conflict with others. I have got plenty of that, but fighting has always been a line I never wanted to cross. If it was necessary then fine, I can confidently defend myself. But fight for no reason? Nope, not me. Fight when there are other logical options? Nope, not me again. It has truly become a last resort.

You may be the opposite of me and that's totally fine, but let me tell you how this fight-avoidant trait has impacted my spiritual life and maybe you can relate to that. See, avoiding a fight is not always the best way out of a conflict. We teach our kids the only way to beat a bully is to stand up for yourself. Well, what happens when the "bully" is your own distorted thoughts, your failing marriage, your childhood trauma, or your hope of a future? Will you fight then? Will you fight for the life that God is calling you to even when it looks different from the one you dreamed of? Will you fight then? Will you fight to push past the pain of trauma and regrets when your heart tries to convince you to stay stuck in unforgiveness? What about when they betray your trust? Will you fight to recover and learn to love again wholeheartedly whether you get the apology or not?

Ladies, THIS is why we must fight. Life has not held back any punches. You've been knocked down by disappointment, grief, abuse, brokenheartedness, and so much more. I thought that as long as I did the right thing and others did the right thing, all the things would be fine. Girl, all the things are not fine. For me, when others didn't do the right thing or even when I didn't do the right thing I subconsciously looked for someone else to save me. I looked for someone else to fight the battle for me because I believed I couldn't. Remember I'm not a fighter or so says the lie I have believed.

Friends, Jesus works on our behalf everyday but He also equips us to fight these battles. No one else is going to save you. But you can do hard things. You can do the thing you dread. You can do the thing no one else believes you can. You can be better, stronger, wiser. Girl, you are a warrior and you must fight!

If that stings a bit you're in good company because when God revealed this to me it was shock and awe for days. But thank God for the Holy Spirit who comforts and guides us. Just as soon as God made it clear that I, the non-fighter, needed to actually fight; He provided the tools and the clarity I needed. I want to share that with you, too.

The "if I must fight" mighty warrior starter package:

1. You have Renewed Strength:

"But they that wait upon the Lord shall renew their strength; they shall mount up with wings as eagles; they shall run, and not be weary; they shall walk, and not faint" Isaiah 40:31 KJV.

Let me be the first to tell you that this truth will make or break the fight. With every battle that we face, we will endure both spiritual and physical strains on our bodies, mind, and spirit. Spiritual fighting takes effort, energy, and time but God has promised to renew our strength. This is a supernatural transaction that can't always be explained in the natural. This is why we pray.

God has the ability to give you the strength, courage, and wisdom you need to fight and win your battles. We can confidently give our all in battle knowing we serve a God who will fight right beside us, not put us on the front line to save himself **(Exodus 14:14)**. No, God is not like that. He's trustworthy. He's gentle. He's a giver. Renewed strength is a promise not a wish. As mighty warriors of God we fight wholeheartedly and receive renewed strength because we put our trust in Him.

2. You have Effective Armor:

You don't go into war alone. Ephesians 6:10-18 explains to us that we have adequate and effective armor. The Breastplate of Righteousness, the Shield of Faith, the Sword of the Spirit, the Gospel Shoes, the Belt of Truth, and the Helmet of Salvation. These all represent the literal protection we can rely on for our most precious parts. In battle God protects our hearts and our minds.

When God saves us we are called to begin the process of mind renewal **(Romans 12:2)**. This is critical. Your mind is the soil of your thoughts and our thoughts turn into actions. Without a renewed mind, we can fall back into old habits simply because our brains are designed to repeat the things we do most. So as we renew our minds with the word of God and create new habits, those truths need to be protected almost like keeping viruses out of a new computer.

God also knows that the success of each battle depends on a guarded heart. *"Guard your heart above all else, for it determines the course of your life"* Proverbs 4:23 NLT.

Our hearts are precious. They need protection in battle. Our hearts are susceptible to internal and external deception. What the heart believes, it does. It's rule over us can make or break our success in battle.

We are equipped with both defensive and offensive tactics. Not only can we utilize our unshakeable Shield of Faith, the foundation on which we believe, but we can also fight back with fiery darts which are the powerful words of God.

3. You have Victory!

"No, despite all these things, overwhelming victory is ours through Christ, who loved us" Romans 8:37 NLT.

You have the victory. Yes, you will have to fight and you may get hurt in the process but in the end you win. Overwhelming victory is ours. It's clearly illustrated throughout scripture from Genesis to Revelation.

- Victory is ours through Christ. 1 Corinthians 15:57
- Victory rests with the Lord. Proverbs 21:31
- The Son appeared to destroy the devil's work. 1 John 3:8
- The Lord is fighting for you. Deuteronomy 3:22
- Not by might, nor by power, but by my Spirit. Zechariah 4:6
- Evil is overcome by good. Romans 12:21
- Enemies will be defeated before you. Deuteronomy 28:7
- No weapon formed against you will prosper. Isaiah 54:17
- Greater is He that is in you. 1 John 4:4
- You have been given authority. Luke 10:19
- God fights for you. Joshua 23:10
- God is with you. Joshua 1:9
- The Blood of the Lamb gives you victory. Revelation 12:11

Whew! That's only a small portion of the truth about our victory in Christ. There is so much more. We are warriors and through Christ we are promised victory. Can I get an Amen?

It's time to put on your big girl panties and do the hard things. We don't have the luxury of taking a back seat to the attacks being launched at us daily. Our families are depending on us. Our future peace is depending on us. Sis, your unhealed inner child that aches with pain, longs to reconcile what happened to her and why; she's depending on you. What happened to you was not your fault. They disappointed you, let you down. Mishandled your trust. They didn't fight for you. They left you hanging. They utterly dropped the ball. It was out of your control then, but you can change things now. You are empowered through Christ.

Forgive, heal, begin again, dream again, hope again, love uninhibitedly because girl you got a mean spiritual left hook and your daddy don't play! Life is hard, but you have nothing to lose when you choose to trust that God is making a warrior out of you. It begins with one punch. One step that says I can do this. God has your back and I believe in you.

You can fight back for all the things that the enemy tries to destroy and steal. You have the tools girlfriend, now prepare for battle; you already know who's gonna win.

Prayer:
Thank You, God for creating in me the power to be a warrior. Help me to embrace that power and receive renewed strength. Teach me how to fight the spiritual and physical battles of this world. God, I believe I have the victory. Thank You for gifts of armor to protect and guide me. I thank You because I can do hard things. Create a fighter in me, Lord, by the power of your Spirit. In Jesus' name, amen.

Highlights:

- We live in spiritual warfare everyday. There's no way around it.
- You can affect the unseen spiritual battles around you. Prayer is a powerful weapon.
- Jesus has given you power and equipped you to fight these battles.
- Avoiding the fight will not exempt you from the battle.
- You must fight to recover from past hurt and trauma to live the life you are called to.
- Jesus has equipped you to fight, no one else will save you from doing hard things.
- As you fight, God promises renewed strength.
- God gives you effective armor for the fight.
- You already have the victory.

Warrior in Action:

- Repeat the following affirmation: "I am a warrior, I can do hard things."
- Make a commitment to yourself to heal. Fight back against all the negative thoughts, habits, actions and traumas of your past. The best way to fight back is to commit to healing. Make a therapy appointment, change your eating habits, ask for forgiveness, move towards forgiving someone, retrain your thoughts according to the word of God. In doing just one of these things, the slow yet rewarding process of healing begins.

Nine

Walk it out

If I told you I started writing this book more than 5 years ago would you believe me? I had the entire outline completed with scriptures to boot. Remember, this book began as a study I led in my Facebook community group in 2015. The feedback and success of the study prompted me to turn it into a book. What if I told you I happen to have 3 other half written books on my Google Drive as we speak. A couple glances at my computer files and you'll see content calendars, yearly plans, speaking pitches, devotional ideas, and incomplete book proposals galore. Girl, I am the queen of unfinished business! But why?

Why is it that I have taken so long to produce something that God birthed inside of me a long time ago? My struggles are the same as yours. My fears are just as present as yours. At times I feel stuck, undesirable, useless, and defeated. I feel pulled and strained by my circumstances. I feel overwhelmed by my responsibilities. I feel unworthy.

Let me be clear. I was stuck. For years. The funny thing is, I didn't even know I was stuck. Sure I was living, going through the motions, making plans to do all the things but honey I was going nowhere. I used to have a recurring dream that I was running from someone but not getting anywhere. No matter how hard I ran I could never quite get away. For all my dream interpreters you already know what this means. My dreams were manifesting what I experienced in real life. It was a real place of uncertainty, a lack of confidence, and the inability to move. Nothing like the plans God has for me.

I knew what God spoke to me years ago. In 2010, God called me into ministry and then in 2014, God told me as plain as day to write my story and share it. It was a simple command. It didn't come with a pdf attached illustrating how I should do that, but given the situation I was dealing with at the time I was certainly crystal clear about what I needed to do. I was afraid. I felt raw, vulnerable, and not sure I could do what God asked of me. It was too real, too honest, too transparent. It was going to take another one of those miracles like in college.

Of course, the one thing I knew was that if anybody could work a miracle it was God. But deep down in my heart, and friends this is hard to say out loud; I didn't believe I could do it. I didn't believe that I actually could do the things God was telling me to do. I am the queen of great ideas. I can out-administrate the best of them any day. It's a gift from Jesus and I gladly boast in Him. I can plan, prepare, and execute your idea and your vision, but sadly I hadn't done the same for myself. I'm full of ideas so that means I'm full of new projects. I've started and started and started and started so many things, great amazing Godly things. But for some reason my motivation is on E, I'm often low on the follow-through and even worse on the finish. It's truly been a struggle trying to reconcile in my mind how I can be so successful in so many areas but lack such belief for myself and my God-given purpose.

My lack of belief has kept me from finishing this one book for 5 years! I haven't trusted God. I haven't believed His truth about Himself let alone His truth about me. I have believed the lie that my circumstances, my healing process, and my procrastination were holding me back. When what I really did was believe that God COULDN'T move my kinda lazy, my kinda overwhelmed, my kinda messy life. I believed for years that my mess was too much. My confidence was too low. My time was too thin. My follow-through was struggling. I have too many kids and way too many bills. My problems will get in the way. I need to get free from drama first, and then I could really concentrate on what God was calling me to do. I used any and every excuse. My inner child's quest for perfection runs deep when all along God wanted to use was my messy, unfinished, imperfect life as ministry.

I have failed at grasping these truths ya'll. Every. Single. One. I write this from a place of humility because I need the same reminders I am giving every day of my life. My brain is wired to notice the bad, the failures, the inconsistencies, and the negative. The way I have seen myself is clearly not the way God sees me.

I find myself needing constant motivation and redirection when it comes to walking out purpose with certainty. What God has called you and I to is a great work. In and out of the home. On and off the stage. With and without the Instagram filter. It's heavy, ladies and the responsibility is real. I don't care if you're in the season of child rearing or retirement and everything in between. You are facing opposition every day because the enemy knows that God has called you to become more.

Friends, let us not get confused. It's not busy work or schedule packing that God has called you to. He's called you to walk in truth and walk out truth. We are to be living testimonies. God's truth will lead you to every door you are meant to walk through. It's already done. But because God wants us to participate in this thing with Him we have a role to play.

You can't begin to fulfill the role God has given you or any role you may have in this life without the full knowledge of God's truth about who you are. Knowing who you are will have you finishing up a book that took you 5 years to complete in one weekend. Yes girl, read that again. I finished this thing up in 2 days flat! I'm learning that God wants us to rest in His power, His Grace, and His Love; not our plans, our efforts, and our own strength.

Solo parenting through a global pandemic was not my idea of a good time when I rang in the New Year at 12 am on January 1, 2020. As difficult as 2020 was there were many jewels that I carry with me from it that I'll cherish for years to come.

As a homeschool mom I was already responsible for my children's education so there were minimal changes to our daily lives when the world first shut down. But a few weeks into the quarantine I began to notice a few changes within my kids. My three beautiful, perfectly spaced out in age, and 100% planned by yours truly (#confessionsofarecoveringperfectionist) daughters were beginning to be affected by all the changes. At 10, 8, and 4 they each had their own responses to not being able to see friends, or go to homeschool PE or gymnastics, or $5 movies on Tuesday; a family favorite. Their disdain for quarantine began to show in different ways. To one it was isolation and a lack of desire to do things that once were important. For another it was acting out if her activity of choice was denied. For another it was a whining fit when siblings couldn't get along.

I knew something needed to be done but honestly I wasn't motivated to do anything. I was experiencing my own level of corona-induced depression and anxiousness about staying safe. I didn't feel like I had the energy to build them up how they needed when I needed the same for myself. Enter King Jesus. Taking the bare minimum of what I can do and making it enough to meet the needs of my growing and very intellectual children. Now, remember I didn't have a lot to give, but I knew I needed to do something. So, while feeling uninspired I took the extra space on my kitchen calendar dry erase board and wrote down some affirmations and feeling statements. I wrote things like: "You are chosen", "You can do hard things", "Take deep breaths when feeling mad". My many years of therapy have taught me that a good old affirmation can be gold on a rough day.

I would write down a few new ones each week and read them off to the girls at the beginning of the week, then I'd usually rush off to do real work like answering emails and laundry. At the bottom of the board I'd always leave a message like "Mom loves you". I didn't really know if they were paying attention. I didn't know if they cared or if what I was doing was helpful. Let me tell you sis, I didn't care to ask them either. Hello overworked and drained quarantined mom syndrome. The truth sometimes sounds terrible on paper but I promised God I would tell it.

In my mind I was like, "Look kids, this is all I got." But to God, that was all that was required of me. Little did I know, my kids were actually paying attention to what I was doing. One day as I was changing the affirmations I looked at the bottom of the board to discover that my I love you message had been responded to. My oldest, Am-Bam, had written me back and said, "We love you too, Mom."

I just about broke down in tears that very moment. They actually were listening. They were paying attention and it meant something. I realized that not only did God take my lack and multiply it to meet the needs of my children whom I often feel like I'm failing because I don't live up to my own expectations of perfection. He took it a step further. Through my obedience of giving just only what I had, God showed my daughters His truth about themselves; that He loves THEM, He cherishes THEM, He is for THEM and not against them. And miraculously through a simple dry erase board they got it! I know they got it because of the response. The acceptance of truth produces action. They received His truth and showed it by passing that same love back to me **(John 13:35)**.

Our children are watching us. They are mimicking our every move. Our faith is not only being tested, but it is also on display to the people we share our lives with daily. Now stay with me because you do not want to miss where I'm going. My children were in need of something, albeit something I didn't have. They needed to be reminded of the truth during the most stressful time of their lives so far and they needed to hear it from the person they trusted most: their mom. Every person reading this right now is in need of something. We have a heavenly Father that lacks nothing and is willing and able to supply all of our needs **(Philippians 4:19)**.

I know a lot of the things you have read in this book are not new ideas. A lot like the things I wrote on my dry erase board for my kids, you've heard these truths before. But if you're anything like my children, something happens when truth is given, heard, and received by someone you trust. And friends I'm not talking about me, I'm talking about God.

God gives us these truths straight from His word. We have two choices; we can either continue to hear His truth and reject it for ourselves by letting it slide in one ear and out of the other;

or we can embrace His truth, let it change our hearts, and show God we get it by passing it on to someone else. That's how the Gospel grows! Remember, God doesn't need us to agree with His truth in order for it to be true. So, rejecting His truth about ourselves only limits our minds, confidence, and esteem. It is still true, we just miss out on it.

Let's take advice from my girls, embrace these truths God has so eloquently displayed for you daily and let your response be in your becoming. Become a walking example of the very truth of Jesus, just as He intended. Become the walking promises of God. Become the example of redemption, hope, and reconciliation. Become undone so that you can become healed by the power of the blood of Jesus.

Believe that you are everything God says you are. Believe that God is everything He says He is. Believe in the virtue that God has given you and share it with the world unapologetically. Believe that it is not over for you. Believe that you are not too far gone, too wrong, too scared, or too stuck. Believe that God is good and all these messy things will work together for your good. Believe that vulnerability, honesty, compassion, and transparency are the new strengths. Leap with each new endeavor, knowing you are not leaping into an unknown abyss but instead the unchanging arms of Jesus. And sis, when life gets you down like I know that it will; rinse, wash, and repeat! Keep on going and doing what is right **(Galatians 6:9)**.

We don't have to feel outshined by the Proverbs 31 woman or anyone's picture perfect social media feeds. She is not our enemy. The same God that makes a way in her life is making a way for you. God's truths never grow old and aren't in danger of being outdated or replaced. We can trust His word.

"God calls us loved, redeemed, chosen, healed, forgiven, set free, pursued, beautiful, special, irreplaceable, warrior, powerful, and the best one is that he calls us HIS."
Kelly Foster

Prayer:

Dear Heavenly Father, You are King of the universe. You completed creation in 6 days, yet You rested on the 7th day. You looked at all You had done and said that it was good. Thank You, God for proclaiming that it was Good. I look to You, Lord, for leadership to complete the impossible in my life. I seek Your face for the wisdom to make Godly choices that improve the lives of everyone I touch. Help me to walk these truths out like only You can. Fill me with power to be a woman of virtue with these truths at the forefront of my heart. In Jesus' name, amen.

Highlights:
- Fulfilling God's plans for you begins with knowing the truth of who you are.
- God gives us these truths; we can either reject them or accept them, but they are still true.
- We show God that we accept His truth about us by becoming all that God intended, not perfectly but persistently.
- We show God that we accept His truth about us by believing that nothing is too hard for God.

Becoming in Action:

- Forgive yourself. Let yourself off the hook. Stop pressuring yourself about where you are and where you think you should be.
- Repeat this affirmation: "I am exactly where I'm supposed to be. God is powerful enough to make up for any setback I've experienced."

Download a complete version of affirmation cards included in this book at Kellyafoster.com/resources

The Real Me?

I t's been quite a journey, hasn't it? I told you I'd be with you the entire way cheering you on as your personal spiritual trainer. Well, at this point we're approaching the end of our time. If you've ever had a personal training session, especially after signing up for that gym membership you never use; then you know a trainer will push you 'til the very end. Welcome to the end, ladies. I'm going to get one last push out of you.

Whenever I write I begin the process in prayer. Nothing I say is worthwhile unless the sweet aroma of Jesus' grace and truth is laced through and through. My hope is that this book will begin a new process for you. A process filled with renewed hope, the truth of your identity in your heart, and the fulfillment of your God-given dreams. Friends, my prayer is that you find R.E.S.T. in Jesus.

Think of the R.E.S.T. acronym as your guide to keep you on the right path after you finish this book. Everything is great while your head is in an encouraging read, but once it's over you practically forget all the great tools you learned. The good thing about R.E.S.T. is that you already know it, I've just condensed the information in an easy to remember acronym so you never forget it.

R. Remember who you are. I can't stress this enough. You are so much more than the sum total of all you've been through. God loves you so much He bought you with the priceless blood of Jesus. Don't let the world and all its problems make you forget who you are. Ever.

E. Engage your barriers, don't run from them. We all have challenges and barriers that impact our ability to walk out virtue and purpose in our lives. These areas are meant to grow you. Use them, don't run from them, pretend they're not there, or dismiss them. They will make you better.

S. Set your passions on fire. When you know who you are and you're no longer afraid of your barriers, imperfections and setbacks- you can start doing. Start doing more of the things you are passionate about. Do the things God is calling you to even if you have to do it afraid. This ignites an unquenchable fire in you to persist, especially when things get hard.

T. Teach yourself to own & live your story. Your story is unique. It makes you the best and only person qualified to do you. So own it and live it. Thrive in the life you have, imperfections and all. This process must be taught, it doesn't come naturally but the benefits of the freedom that comes from it are so worth it.

When you close this book you can walk away knowing that all you have to do is R.E.S.T in Jesus. All the principles, truths, and key ideas point back to Christ. He is and will always be our rest and refuge.

Now for the challenge. I can't end this book without challenging you, without pushing you, not only to finish but to finish well. Why? Because that's what a good trainer does.

I began praying a prayer a few years ago. I was in the middle of the hardest moment of my life. My marriage was failing and it looked like the metaphorical plug would need to be pulled. I was confused about everything. I recognized that I was changing because of all the things I had been through. I was erecting walls and building divisions within myself. I was becoming snarky, numb, distrusting, and mean. I understand now that I was guarding myself because of the unbearable pain; an ineffective but often used form of self-protection. I knew I couldn't stop it on my own. I didn't like this new person I was turning into. So at the urging of a few great accountability partners I decided to intensely and specifically pray about it. In this prayer, which started small but eventually took on a life all on it's own; I asked God to change me. I needed God to make me the woman I'm supposed to be instead of the one I felt like life made me.

I'm going to go all the way out on a limb here and share my prayer. I call it The Miracle Prayer. I love to lead by example; I think it's one of the most effective ways to reach the heart of people. Remember, I'm from the Show Me State. So as you read my prayer, just know that your spiritual coach is eventually going to push you to write a prayer of your own. Ok, here goes:

"Dear Lord of Mercy and Father of Comfort, You are the One I turn to for help in moments of weakness and times of need. I ask you to be with me now in this time of healing and recovery.

Psalm 107:20 says that you send out your Word and heal your people. So then, please send Your healing Word to me now. In the name of Jesus, drive out all brokenness and affliction from this body. God help me to find victory in my own journey. Help me to seek Your perfect love that is patient and kind.

Dear Lord, I ask You to turn my weakness into strength, my suffering into compassion, sorrow into joy, and pain into comfort for others.

May I, Your servant, trust in Your goodness and hope in Your faithfulness, even in the middle of this struggle. Lord, help me to trust Your word over what my feelings and circumstances say.

Fill me with patience and joy in Your presence as I breathe in Your healing life.

Please restore me to wholeness. Remove all fear and doubt from my heart by the power of Your Holy Spirit, and may You, Lord, be glorified in my life. Help me to understand that grace anchors me. Remove the chemical bonds that tie me to unsafe and unhealthy situations. Loose the bonds now, God in Jesus' name. As You heal and renew me, Lord, may I bless and praise You. Lord help me to expose the darkness of my soul to the light of Your presence every single day.

Help me to see You, help me to experience Your grace, help me to feel Your presence in everything I do. Help me to live each day with a heart of thankfulness. Reveal the aroma of Your sweet presence to my dying flesh. Renew me, fill me up with Your Spirit. Give me strength and wisdom to separate myself from codependent behaviors. Lead my path towards healthy decisions.

Protect me from myself, God. Help me to make tough decisions and to stick with healing at all costs.

God, bear the weight of this pain, bring me joy and a new song in the morning. Help me to find You in my mourning and joy in my sufferings. Still my heart with Your peace, comfort my wounds with Your healing balm. Rebuild in me everything that is broken, restore, refresh, and renew me. Prepare me for the new thing You are doing.

Lord be my rock, my song, and my salvation. Create in me a clean heart. Fill every void in my heart. Help me to move forward into a new life in Christ with assurance of Your provision, faithfulness, and love. I believe that You are good, that You have been good to me and that even through this situation You are working for my good. Create a new woman in me, make me a kinder, gentler, more loving soul that draws others to you through grace, love, and compassion.

All of this, I pray in the name of Jesus Christ. Amen."

Sadly, this wasn't the first time I began to change. I remember the very moment that I began to become someone else other than who I was meant to be in Christ. It's a silly story but clearly defines the beginning of my hardened heart. I was 6 years old, it was a Saturday morning and I was getting ready to go to a birthday party. It was 1990 so birthday parties were a big deal. This was back when everyone dressed up for parties. All the girls wore their party dresses and the boys would even wear slacks. My mom had just finished getting me ready and she was beginning to put herself together in the bathroom.

I was so excited about this party. I even got to pick out my dress. I wore my white ruffle dress with red and black polka dots with the matching bolero. You would have thought it was Chanel how proud I was to wear it. My legs were freshly oiled and shining from the vaseline my mom used. I had on pretty white ruffle socks to match and my dainty black patent leather shoes with just a touch of a heel to make me feel that sass I still crave to this day. I was cute and I felt cute. My big poofy hair had been slicked into a high side ponytail. I was looking good by the 90's kindergarten standard and I was over the moon excited about showing off my good looks at the party.

Well, fast forward a bit because things get fuzzy when you're telling a 30-year-old story. As I waited for my mother to finish getting ready, my older sister Niccole who had to be 8 or 9 at the time decided she was going to run away. Now let me be clear, this child was not actually going to run away. Apparently, everyone in the house knew this but me. She was being a kid, looking for attention, and her next prank victim. I was it.

At 6, I remember being so loving, so compassionate, so caring towards everyone. I distinctly remember feeling open, trusting, and viewing the world through these fresh eyes. I wasn't afraid. I believed what people told me and I trusted that they wanted the best for me. So when my sister said she was running away I actually believed her. The last thing I wanted was for her to leave. I loved her. Next thing I know I am chasing her out the door and down the street in my white ruffle dress and black patent leather shoes with the kitten heel.

I was the only person chasing her. "Stop, stop, don't run away," I remember yelling to her. She kept going and probably was laughing the entire time. 2 minutes later, I'm in the street with a dusty dress and busted knees. Yep, I slipped and fell and banged up my knees really bad. I still bear these scars today, y'all. When she saw me down, she quickly turned around and helped me limp back to the house.

There's something about hitting the concrete full force that knocks something out of you. All of a sudden it all made sense. The joke was literally on me. I realized she was never going to run away and had just been messing with her gullible and impressionable younger sister.

I was hot. I mean I was really mad. Here I am looking fly as I can be, wearing my favorite dress getting ready to go to the party and now I have two bloody busted knees. Of course that meant I needed an outfit change because my knees looked like I got dressed in the back of a butcher shop. I still wanted to go to the party so I settled for ripped jeans and a cropped top. Did I mention I love the 90's? Life was so simple. To top it all off my mom, being the ultimate MacGyver, made me homemade bandages for my knees. Homemade bandages people, way to add insult to injury. So we were off to the party. I ended up being the only one in jeans and it crushed my 6-year-old party dreams. I think I began hating my sister that day. Ok, not exactly I'm only kidding.

But something did happen to me that day. I learned a lesson that would follow me all my life; it changed me. Seeds of distrust, sarcasm, anger, and insecurity were planted that day. My inner child stopped growing just a bit. I learned that sometimes you can be serious while others are playing with you and their actions might end up costing you. This was one memorable moment but there are many that came after that. These situations feed on trauma and give it the appearance of truth. As these situations repeat over time the lie becomes reality to us.

I learned that the world couldn't handle me. The world didn't know what to do with the natural compassion, love, and gentleness God placed on the inside of me. So I did what most of us do to survive; I changed. I changed who I really was and became a person who couldn't be fooled, couldn't be tricked, duped, or misled by people of this world. But it also meant that I couldn't be fully loved, known, or even protected by a Holy God. I didn't know how to continue to be the real me and survive in a world that mishandled me at every point.

Maybe you've done the same thing. Maybe you've traveled so far from the real you, the you God made you to be. The you that knew she was loved, cherished, powerful, beautiful, irreplaceable, pursued, full of purpose, and a warrior. At one point you were fearless before you learned that someone could take advantage of you. At one point you were confident in who you were before someone tried to convince you that different was better. Sis, it's time to get back to the real you.

I've clearly illustrated just how important you are to Jesus. You're empowered with His word as proof, but if you don't agree to leave that old you behind and embrace the you God made you to be from the beginning you'll be right back where you began. This work is a journey and it won't be finished once you close this book. As mother Iyanla would say, "Beloved, you've got to do your work." I promise you, although long and daunting at times, fully embracing who you are in Christ is a work that will completely change your life.

So now friend, it's time to begin your own prayer. Don't think of this as a one-time prayer, think of it as an ongoing conversation. Start small and gradually build upon it over time. Write it down. That's very important. Read it every day. Trust me, once you start this prayer God will give you words to add to it daily. You'll see scriptures that you want to add and people you will want to include. As things come up in your life that you are struggling with, be it lack of confidence, insecurity, loneliness, or fear; God will give you a word to combat it in prayer. Use the scriptures as your power in this prayer. Praying scripture is the best way to stay aligned with God's will. He loves when we remind Him of what He's said.

So as you remember that you are loved, pursued, powerful, beautiful, irreplaceable, forgiven, and a warrior, know that you are honoring the God who called you this first. We owe it to Him and to ourselves to become the women He created us to be. Nothing less will do.

~

Writing The Miracle Prayer: You can find a template at Kellyafoster.com/resources

Take a moment. Sit still and listen to the quiet peace of your breath. Now begin. Begin to write down your prayer to God. Put it in something you can easily grab at a moment's notice. When God gives you a scripture to add or words to say you want it to be handy. I use the notes app on my phone.

Pray that He returns you back to the woman you were always meant to be. Use your own words. It doesn't have to be profound because it's personal. Pray for His protection as you release control and knock down the walls you've built to "protect" yourself. Pray specifically for those things that you long for in your heart. Those things that you've lost hope in, yep, include all of those things. Commit to adding to this prayer for the next year. You can add to it as the Holy Spirit leads you, there are no winners and this is not a race. But don't short change yourself. Inch by inch as you add to it and pray it everyday you'll begin to see God change your heart and your mind. First towards yourself and then towards others. Consider this a gift to yourself. You're worth it.

And just like that you made it to the end of this workout but the journey still continues. You now have everything you need to successfully walk out virtuous womanhood just as Christ intended. No longer are you held back by your past or paralyzed in fear by your future. Equipped with these 7 truths, the sky's the limit for your spiritual growth. I pray that you feel motivated, encouraged, and fired up to live out God's truth in your life everyday. Blessings, friend!

THANKS FOR READING!

Now you can be the first to hear about new book releases, events and classes from Kelly A. Foster and the women's ministry, Imperfectly His.

Follow me on 📘 📷 🐦 @_Kellyafoster @imperfectlyhis

GRAB YOUR BOOK BONUSES

Every purchase of this book allows you exclusive access to our book resources page which includes:

- The Official Dear Proverbs 31 Woman Study Guide
- BEAUTIFUL Prayer guide
- The Miracle Prayer Template
- And SO much more!

www.KellyAFoster.com/resources
Use password DP31

LEAVE AN AMAZON REVIEW

The best way to help others find this book is to let them know how it impacted you by WRITING A REVIEW on Amazon.

SUBSCRIBE TO BECOME A BESTIE

My subscribers are known as my BESTIES because they get the best of me! I'd love for you to be my newest bestie. Use the link below to subscribe to receive exclusive updates, new book excerpts, devotionals and content to keep you healthy, whole and healed.

www.subscribepage.com/kellyafoster